Shrubs to Know
in Pacific Northwest Forests

This book is dedicated to all of my students — past, present and future —
who continually help me remember who I wanted to be when I was young.

Edward C. Jensen
Author and photographer

Oregon State University
Extension Service

EC 1640 • Revised April 2022

Cover photo by Edward C. Jensen, ninebark, *Physocarpus capitatus*
Book and cover design by Janet Donnelly
Illustrations by Erik Simmons
Maps by David A. Zahler and Alan Dennis
Photos by Edward C. Jensen unless otherwise noted
Photo editing by David A. Zahler and Erik Simmons

ORDERING INFORMATION

Visit catalog.extension.oregonstate.edu or call 1-800-561-6719

Oregon State University Extension Service
422 Kerr Administration Building
Corvallis, OR 97331
catalog.extension.oregonstate.edu

ISBN-13: 978-0-87071-320-0
Library of Congress Control Number:
2022936600

Extension work is a cooperative program of Oregon State University, the U.S. Department of Agriculture, and Oregon counties. Oregon State University Extension Service offers educational programs, activities, and materials without discrimination on the basis of race, color, national origin, religion, sex, gender identity (including gender expression), sexual orientation, disability, age, marital status, familial/parental status, income derived from a public assistance program, political beliefs, genetic information, veteran's status, reprisal or retaliation for prior civil rights activity. (Not all prohibited bases apply to all programs.) This publication will be made available in an accessible alternative format upon request. Please contact puborders@oregonstate.edu or 1-800-561-6719.

The Library of Congress has cataloged the 2013 edition as follows:

Jensen, Edward C.
  Shrubs to know in Pacific Northwest forests / author and photographer, Edward C. Jensen ; range maps and photo selection, David A. Zahler.
    p. cm. — (EC ; 1640)
    ISBN 978-0-87071-320-0
    1. Shrubs—Northwest, Pacific—Identification. 2. Forest plants—Northwest, Pacific—Identification. I. Zahler, David A. II. Oregon State University. Extension Service. III. Title. IV. Series: EC (Oregon State University. Extension Service) ; 1640.
QK144.J46 2013
582.16—dc23

2013032254

Contents

■ Introduction 5

■ Key to shrubs and vines 26

■ List of shrubs 34

  Acer MAPLE 34
  Alnus ALDER 36
  Amelanchier SERVICEBERRY 38
  Arctostaphylos MANZANITA 39
  Artemisia SAGEBRUSH 43
  Bacharris COYOTEBRUSH 44
  Berberis BARBERRY, OREGON-GRAPE 45
  Betula BIRCH 48
  Ceanothus CEANOTHUS 49
  Celtis HACKBERRY 56
  Cercocarpus MOUNTAIN-MAHOGANY 57
  Chrysolepis CHINQUAPIN 59
  Clematis CLEMATIS 60
  Cornus DOGWOOD 61
  Corylus HAZELNUT 62
  Crataegus HAWTHORN 63
  Cytisus BROOM 65
  Dasiphora SHRUBBY CINQUEFOIL 66
  Ericameria GOLDENBUSH, RABBITBRUSH 67
  Garrya SILKTASSEL 68
  Gaultheria SALAL 70
  Holodiscus OCEANSPRAY 71
  Juniperus JUNIPER 72
  Lonicera HONEYSUCKLE 73
  Malus APPLE, CRABAPPLE 77
  Menziesia MENZIESIA 78
  Myrica SWEETGALE, BAYBERRY 79
  Oemleria OEMLERIA, INDIAN-PLUM 80
  Oplopanax OPLOPANAX, DEVILSCLUB 81
  Paxistima PAXISTIMA, BOXWOOD 82
  Philadelphus MOCKORANGE 83
  Physocarpus NINEBARK 84
  Prunus CHERRY, PLUM 85
  Purshia BITTERBRUSH 88
  Rhamnus BUCKTHORN 89
  Rhododendron RHODODENDRON, AZALEA 91
  Ribes CURRANT, GOOSEBERRY 94
  Rosa ROSE 102
  Rubus BLACKBERRY 104
  Salix WILLOW 110
  Sambucus ELDERBERRY 112
  Shepherdia BUFFALOBERRY 114
  Sorbus MOUNTAIN-ASH 115
  Spiraea SPIREA 117
  Symphoricarpos SNOWBERRY 119
  Toxicodendron POISONOAK, POISONIVY 121
  Ulex GORSE 123
  Vaccinium BLUEBERRY, HUCKLEBERRY 124
  Viburnum VIBURNUM 134

■ Resources 136

■ Checklist and index 137

Redstem ceanothus, *Ceanothus sanguinea*

What to know about
Shrubs to Know

This book is intended as a companion to *Trees to Know in Oregon and Washington*, an Oregon State University Extension Service mainstay since its initial publication in 1950. Here's what you'll find in *Shrubs to Know*:

- **New in the 2022 edition:** At the suggestion of readers, two species have been added: western poisonivy *(Toxicodendron rydbergii)* and bush chinkapin *(Chrysolepis sempervirens)*. This also required several changes to the key.

- **This book includes shrubs** that grow in and around forests. Some species also grow in rangelands, in generally nonforested valleys or above the tree line, but all have a strong connection to forests.

- **Geographically, it covers** most of the Pacific Northwest — Oregon, Washington, northern California, southern British Columbia, the panhandle of Idaho and adjoining parts of western Montana. Many species in the book range even more widely than this.

- **Most shrubs described in this book** are native, but some are naturalized. (Humans introduced them, but they escaped cultivation and now survive on their own.) All grow and reproduce without human intervention. There are far too many native and naturalized shrubs to include, so I selected about 100 as a starting point. This book does not cover ornamental and horticultural species, except for natives that are used in that fashion.

- **The Pacific Northwest is home** to many shrubs that grow tall enough to be considered trees (although they typically have multiple stems) and a few that sometimes grow with a single stem (like a tree). As a result, some species included in this book are also covered in *Trees to Know in Oregon and Washington*, but I have tried to minimize the overlap.

- **Most shrubs in this book** are described at the species level, but several are described at the subspecies or variety level when it seems more appropriate. Two group entries (for *Rosa* and *Salix*) emphasize genus-level characteristics rather than species characteristics because the characteristics separating species are often minor or intergrade between species.

- **Shrubs in this book** are arranged alphabetically by scientific name (genus and species). I believe most readers will find this easier than arrangement by a larger taxonomic category, such as family.

I hope you'll find using *Shrubs to Know* easy and fun. If you do, my time has been well spent. Now, go out and enjoy our forests — and take a friend with you!

— Edward C. Jensen

Companion volume

Learn to identify the trees around you with *Trees to Know in Oregon and Washington*. To order, visit catalog.extension.oregonstate.edu or call 1-800-561-6719.

Two shrubs to know before you go: Pacific poisonoak and western poisonivy

Don't go into the woods before learning to identify these common plants.
Exposure to Pacific poisonoak or western poisonivy provokes uncomfortable allergic reactions.
Here's what you need to know.

Pacific poisonoak 'leaves of three'

PHOTO: JOE MONTGOMERY

Western poisonivy

What they have in common

- **Both cause severe skin allergies in most people.** Both are members of the genus *Toxicodendron*, all members of which share a chemical called urushiol, to which most humans are allergic. This chemical is present in all parts of the plant, during all seasons of the year. It can be transferred to humans by touch, via clothes or pet fur and even from the smoke of burning plants. Learn to recognize both of these plants so you can avoid them altogether. And, try to wear long shirts and pants.

- **Both have pinnately compound leaves,** most commonly with three leaflets per leaf. Occasionally, poisonoak has five leaflets per leaf, but poisonivy does not. The three-leaved nature of both species has given rise to the saying "leaves of three, let it be."

- **Both grow as bushy shrubs,** but poisonoak also has the ability grow as a sprawling or climbing vine. Western poisonivy does not.

- **Both spread by seeds,** but also by underground stems, called rhizomes. In fact, rhizomes are the primary way they spread, and why they typically grow in dense clumps.

- **Both have leaves that turn** yellow, orange or brilliant red in the fall — but don't pick them for your floral arrangements!

- **Both have fruits with a single hard seed** growing in dangling clusters. Each seed is enclosed in a greenish, yellowish or whitish papery husk. They often resemble tiny pumpkins.

- **Neither is what it sounds like.** Poisonoak is not really an oak (or even related to oaks), and poisonivy is not a true ivy. As a result, the common names are typically written as one word or hyphenated.

Pacific poisonoak

Western poisonivy

What they don't share

- **Location, location, location.** Pacific poisonoak grows primarily at low elevations west of the Cascades and Sierra Nevadas — both in dry forests and open fields. Western poisonivy grows east of the Cascades and Sierra Nevadas, primarily along streams and rivers, especially in the dry Intermountain West. It stretches across much of Canada and the United States to the eastern seaboard. There, it merges with and hybridizes with eastern poisonivy. The only place poisonoak and poisonivy occur together is on dry sites in the Columbia Gorge, primarily around Cascades Locks.

- **Growth form:** Both grow as bushy shrubs. Pacific poisonoak is sometimes called a "shape-shifter" because it also grows as a sprawling vine, both along the ground and reaching high into trees.

These species are described in more detail on pages 121 and 122.

Pacific poisonoak grows as both a low shrub and a sprawling vine that climbs high into trees.

What is a shrub?

The distinction between trees and shrubs is often intuitively clear. But when shrubs grow as large as they do in the Pacific Northwest, and as their forms change to match their environments, the distinction sometimes blurs.

Here's a basic definition of shrubs:

- **Shrubs are woody, perennial plants.** They have woody stems and roots, and they typically live several decades, or much longer in some cases.

- **Shrubs typically have multiple stems,** but some shrubs may have a short, single trunk, and some trees commonly sprout from the base and so also have multiple trunks.

- **Shrubs are typically less than 20 feet tall** at maturity, although some may grow much taller in the right environments.

- **Shrubs typically have main stems** that are less than 6 inches in diameter when measured 4.5 feet above the ground (commonly called breast height), although some may grow much larger in the right environments.

- **Shrubs often have characteristic shapes** when they grow in the open. In the forest, shrubs have diverse shapes influenced by the environments in which they grow.

So, follow this basic definition but don't be overly concerned about its strict application.

Shrubs are vital components of Pacific Northwest forests. They are integral to these forests' many uses and values — including wood, water, wildlife, biodiversity, ethnobotany, and recreation — and absolutely critical to how these forests function ecologically.

Bitterbrush grows against the orange bark of a ponderosa pine. Shrubs typically have multiple stems, while trees have single trunks.

Perceptions of shrubs often depend on who is using the forest for what purposes. Shrubs can certainly impede walking and working in the woods, but they also add color and vibrancy to a fall hike. They compete with desired tree species for water and growing space, but they also contribute vital nutrients to the soil. Shrubs provide food and shelter for wildlife but can make hunting a difficult process. Some shrubs have commercial value in their own right, while others impede the development of commercial value of other species. As a result, our relationship with forest shrubs is often one of mixed emotions. Whether you consider them friend or foe (or both, depending on the circumstances), it's good and useful to know the shrubs that occupy our forests.

Be a shrub detective

Identifying shrubs is a lot like identifying people. You can easily recognize a close friend, even if you catch only a glimpse. In fact, you can often recognize a friend from a fast-moving car, or even from a picture in a photo album when the friend was a different age or had a different appearance. However, if you meet a room full of strangers, you need to concentrate on specific characteristics before you can begin to tell individuals apart. And even then, you may struggle to remember their names.

It's the same with shrubs and other forest plants. When you know a shrub well, you'll be able to identify and name it whether you see its leaves, its fruit, its flowers or even its shape and color. When you know it well enough, you'll be able to recognize it in different growth stages, in different locations and even from fast-moving cars. You're likely to start by learning its common name but may eventually want to learn its formal or scientific name, which is written in Latin.

How can you get to know shrubs that well? First, learn to identify their most important characteristics, such as leaves, flowers and fruit. As you become better acquainted, examine each shrub more carefully. Look at its bark, branching pattern, color, and shape. Eventually, you may even get to know shrubs by where they live.

This book can help you start to know common forest shrubs. Keep it handy and take it with you on hikes. You'll be surprised how easy it is to learn common shrubs — and how much fun it is to improve your ability each time out.

How can you get to know shrubs? First, learn to identify the most important characteristics, such as leaves, flowers and fruits.

You can improve your ability to identify shrubs each time you visit the forest.

Common and scientific names of shrubs

Plant names can be confusing until you understand how they're developed. All plants have two kinds of names: common names and scientific names. Common names are written in English in English-speaking countries, in German in Germany, in Chinese in China and so on. Scientific names are always written in Latin, so they can be used anywhere in the world.

Scientific names are governed by strict rules set by the International Botanical Congress. In theory, each plant has only one accepted scientific name. However, taxonomists sometimes differ over what scientific name should be applied to a particular plant, so there may be more than one name in use at the same time for the same plant. These are referred to as synonyms — different names for the same plant. Also, some taxonomists are "lumpers" (they prefer to group as many plants together as they can), and others are "splitters" (they prefer to separate plants on the basis of smaller characteristics). This results in differences of opinion about what a particular plant should be called; synonyms also come into play here.

> Taxonomists sometimes differ over what scientific name should be applied to a particular plant.

Common names are usually easier to remember and use than scientific names, but they are developed much differently. Common names are derived in many ways: a characteristic of the plant (vine maple or thinleaf alder), the geographic location in which it grows (Pacific serviceberry or Rocky Mountain maple), the area where it was first identified and categorized by Euro-Americans (Sierra gooseberry or Sitka alder), the habitat in which it grows (bog blueberry or mountain huckleberry) or a person's name (Douglas spirea or Fremont's silktassel), to name but a few.

There are few rules for assigning common names, and no one determines which common names are correct. Most often, local conventions rule. A plant can have many common names, and these names may reflect different countries or regions, growth stages, uses, or growth characteristics. For example, ponderosa pine is also called western yellow pine, bull pine, blackjack pine, rock pine, *pinabete, pino real,* and pondosa pine among others. However, its scientific name is always *Pinus ponderosa.* The shrub *Vaccinium membranaceum* is called thinleaf huckleberry, mountain huckleberry, black huckleberry, blue huckleberry, big huckleberry, big huck, square-twig huckleberry, mountain blueberry, mountain bilberry, twin-leaved huckleberry and big whortleberry. Some of these names are also applied to related species, which adds to the confusion of common names.

Plants belong to many different categories, or taxa. The study of taxa is called taxonomy, and people who study taxonomy are called taxonomists. The most commonly used taxa for identifying trees and shrubs are genus and species. A genus is composed of species with similar characteristics, and a family is composed of genera with similar characteristics. All species can also be subdivided into varieties (var.) or subspecies (ssp.). Although the distinction between varieties and subspecies is useful for taxonomists, it is confusing to most others. In this book, varieties and subspecies are mentioned only when they are dominant in the region, and no specific distinction is made between the two taxa.

A scientific name for a species has two parts: the genus followed by a specific epithet (species name). The genus refers to the general type of plant, and the specific epithet refers to one particular species within that genus. For example, the genus for maple is *Acer,* and the specific epithet for vine maple is *circinatum,* so the scientific name for the vine maple species is *Acer circinatum.* Because it always has two parts, this type of name is called a Latin binomial.

Douglas maple

How common and scientific names fit together

Type of name	Genus	Specific epithet	Species name
Common name	maple	Douglas	Douglas maple
Scientific name	*Acer*	*glabrum* var. *douglasii*	*Acer glabrum* var. *douglasii*

Common names generally work the same way. In the case of vine maple, "maple" refers to the genus, and "vine maple" refers to the particular species of maple.

Other maples have the same genus name but different species names. For example:

BIGLEAF MAPLE: *Acer macrophyllum*

ROCKY MOUNTAIN MAPLE: *Acer glabrum*

DOUGLAS MAPLE (a particular variety of Rocky Mountain maple): *Acer glabrum* var. *douglasii*

However, some common names have only one word (snowbrush), and some have more than two (western wayfaring tree). Hyphenated common names indicate that the plant is not what its name implies. Examples from the tree world include Douglas-fir, which is not a fir (firs are in the genus *Abies*, but Douglas-firs are in the genus *Pseudotsuga*), and incense-cedar, which is not a cedar (cedars are in the genus *Cedrus*, but incense-cedar is in the genus *Calocedrus*). Examples from the shrub world include poisonoak, which is not an oak (oaks are in the genus *Quercus*, but poisonoak is in the genus *Toxicodendron*), and Indian-plum, which is not a plum (plums are in the genus *Prunus*, but Indian-plum is in the genus *Oemleria*). Sometimes hyphens are omitted and the two words are joined together if they are easy to read that way. Poisonoak and poison-oak are both correct, but poison oak is not (it implies that the plant is a particular kind of oak, which it is not).

Although this naming system can take a while to get used to, you'll soon realize that learning plant names can be fun. They often tell you something special about the plant, such as who discovered it, a particular characteristic, or where it grows. When you encounter a new plant, see what you can learn from its name.

Native, naturalized, invasive, ornamental — what does it all mean?

- **Native plants** are those that inhabit an area without having been brought there by humans. Some may have developed in a particular location; others may have migrated from surrounding areas in response to natural influences such as climate change or the rise and fall of mountain ranges. Endemic is a more formal word for native and means the same thing.

- **Naturalized plants** are those that have been introduced into an area by humans and, once there, have been able to survive and reproduce on their own without human assistance. Naturalized plants are often referred to as exotics.

- **Invasive plants** are naturalized plants that spread rapidly, often overwhelming native plants. Sometime native plants that rapidly expand their range into new areas — perhaps as a result of human-caused changes — are also said to be invasive. One example is western juniper, which invades native grasslands where humans have suppressed fires.

- **Ornamental plants** are those that humans find useful in beautifying their own managed environments. Ornamentals can be endemic or exotic. Depending on the species and environment, they can also be highly invasive or remain where they are planted.

What is range?

RANGE describes the geographic area over which a shrub occurs. It's often described in terms of geographic boundaries, such as states and countries, or natural barriers, such as oceans, major rivers and mountain ranges. Ranges described in this book are indicators of where you can expect to find specific shrubs, but they do not imply absolute locations.

What is habitat?

HABITATS are types of places within larger geographic ranges where you can expect to find certain shrubs — along a stream, on a dry ridge, or on well-drained soils, for example. Some species have specific requirements and occur only on sites that meet those requirements; these are often referred to as niche-specific species. Other species can grow under a wide range of conditions; these are said to have wide ecological amplitude. Habitat information is often helpful in identifying shrubs. Experience will help you use this information successfully.

Traditional uses of native plants

How people who came before us used plants is often of great interest to those who love native plants. Though I'm not an expert in that field, I've tried to share some information from published literature on how Indigenous people and early settlers of the Pacific Northwest used (and often still use) native plants. Both groups used native plants for food, medicine, clothing, tools and other necessities of daily living. Uses for particular plants often varied widely, especially for widespread shrubs.

Although many people may have used the same plant for medicine, they may have used it in different ways and at different dosages. In fact, it may have been helpful at one dose but harmful at a higher dose.

I strongly recommend against experimenting with medicinal use of plants unless you're with an expert. Because of space limitations, I've greatly simplified what could be long and varied lists of uses of native plants, picking items that seem like they might be of interest.

How shrubs reproduce and respond to fire

The ability of plants to reproduce is crucial to their success in nature. All shrubs can reproduce sexually (from seeds), but some are far more successful at it than others. The type of fruit produced, its abundance and how it's distributed are all important to successful reproduction. Germination and early survival are also critical. Some species need a cold, moist period to germinate; others need exposure to heat or digestion by an animal; others need exposure to a certain light regime.

Most shrubs can also reproduce vegetatively (for example, by sprouting or layering). Depending on the species, shrubs may sprout from the base (where the top of the plant joins the root system), roots, underground burls or underground stems called rhizomes.

Many shrubs also have the ability to layer, which means that new roots and stems form on branches that bend over, touch the ground and become buried.

How plants respond to fire is of increasing interest to those who seek to understand how both managed and unmanaged forest ecosystems function. In general, fire damages the aboveground portions of woody plants, but some plants are more resistant to fire than

Chokecherry sprouts from rhizomes after a fire.

others. The underground portions respond in a variety of ways, ranging from death to very aggressive sprouting from root collars, burls, roots and rhizomes.

The response of plants to fire often determines the species composition and structure of forested landscapes for many decades.

In this book, basic information on reproduction and response to fire is included in the "Notes" section of species descriptions. Other published resources provide more extensive information on this topic.

Red elderberries are edible when cooked but toxic if eaten raw.

Is it edible? Pause and think

USE CAUTION when eating or even tasting unfamiliar plants. Some are delicious, but others can give you an allergic reaction or make you violently ill. Some are toxic when eaten raw but edible when cooked. Some toxic plants resemble others that are edible. You'd miss much of the joy of native plants by never eating any of them, so the species descriptions in this book often include notes about edibility. But again, taste with caution until you're positive about the identity of a plant.

Forest and shrub communities of the Pacific Northwest

Several major factors influence the development of forests and the shrub communities within them:

- **The climate** in which the forest exists.

- **Soils** on which the forest develops.

- **Topography,** which helps determine factors such as soil depth, solar radiation and evapotranspiration.

- **Plants and animals** that occur in the forest and how they interact with each other.

- **Type, severity and frequency of disturbances** such as fire, wind, volcanism, glaciation, and insect and disease epidemics.

An additional factor that influences forest composition is the origin and development of the community of major flora from which the tree and shrub species have come. Forest and range plants currently in the Pacific Northwest arrived here from several substantially different locations. Therefore, they represent substantially different floras. Sometimes the differences in flora are represented by different species in the same genera. In other cases, entirely new genera and families are introduced from different flora. And, of course, many plants cross these theoretical boundaries and are found in more than one forest type.

Four major plant migration routes that contributed to the current forests of the Northwest included:

- Plants that migrated east across the Bering land bridge and then south through Alaska and Greenland.

- Plants originating in Mexico and parts of Central America migrated north along the Rocky and Sierra Nevada mountains, and then into the Pacific Northwest.

- Many plants migrated north from the deserts and high plains of Mexico through the arid lands between the Rocky and Sierra Nevada Mountains.

- And, largely prior to the formation of the many mountain ranges of the American West, plants migrated west from the deciduous forests of eastern North America.

Pacific forests

Rocky Mountain forests

Sierran forests

Approximate area covered by this book

Shaded areas indicate forested lands. Most species described in this book occcur within forests or on their borders; several venture into adjoining rangelands. Some species range more widely than the area shown; others are contained entirely within it.

Pacific forests

Pacific forests occupy the cool, moist forestlands that extend from Kodiak, Alaska, south through the redwood forests of northern California. In Oregon and Washington, these forests occur west of the Cascade crest. But they also extend east across southern British Columbia into parts of northern Idaho and western Montana and south into the coastal ranges of California.

These forests developed in Alaska and Greenland millions of years ago when the earth was warmer and wetter, and migrated south as the planet's climate cooled and vast glaciers formed in the northern polar region. Today, these forests are dominated by evergreen conifers, especially Douglas-fir, western hemlock, western redcedar, Sitka spruce and grand fir at low to mid elevations. At higher elevations, they are dominated by mountain hemlock, noble fir, subalpine fir and Pacific silver fir.

Conifers dominate Pacific forests, along with a diverse mix of shrubs.

The shrub communities in these forests are typically dense, lush, diverse and dominated by many species that reach sizeable proportions. Many species of shrubs exist in these forests. Some of the most common and widespread include salal, rhododendron, vine maple, devilsclub, Pacific serviceberry, snowberry, willows of all sorts, several species of shrubby alders and elderberries, and many species of huckleberries, roses, blackberries, and currants and gooseberries. Many species of ferns, herbs and mosses also inhabit the lush forest floor.

Sierran forests

The Sierran forests that inhabit southwestern Oregon and much of western California between the Coast Ranges and Sierra Nevada are part of a flora that developed in northwestern Mexico and migrated north through western and coastal California. These forests are composed of trees that are smaller in stature and higher in drought tolerance than those occurring farther north. The forests are typically more open and parklike than the dense conifer forests farther north. At lower and drier elevations, they commonly take the form of oak-dominated woodlands rather than closed forests. At higher elevations, conifers dominate the forests, but broadleaved trees are more common than farther north.

Broadleaved trees and conifers populate Sierran forests.

Although there are many tree species in these forests, the characteristic species of the mid- to high-elevation conifer forests include sugar pine, Jeffrey pine, ponderosa pine, white fir, California red fir, incense-cedar, tanoak, Pacific madrone and golden chinkapin. Farther south, in the central Sierras, giant sequoias join this mix. Low to mid elevations in California are dominated by oak woodlands that include several species of pines and many species of oaks that occur exclusively or primarily in California. Of the many Californian oaks, only Oregon white oak, California black oak and canyon live oak occur north of the California–Oregon border.

Again, there are many species of shrubs in these forests. Some common and widespread species include poisonoak, California buckthorn, birchleaf and curlleaf mountain-mahogany, and many species of manzanita, ceanothus and roses. In the lower, drier rangelands east of the Sierras, big sagebrush, gray rabbitbrush and bitterbrush are common; these species are also common east of the Cascades north through Oregon and Washington into British Columbia and east into Idaho.

Rocky Mountain forests

The Rocky Mountain forests found east of the Cascades and stretching into the Rockies are most heavily influenced by the Rocky Mountain flora, although they typically include species from both the Pacific and Sierran forests. The diversity of species is particularly high in these forests for a variety of reasons: the great elevation gradients involved, the largely unbroken string of mountains running north to south, a rich and varied geological history, a long history of volcanism and glaciation, a diverse fire history and the diversity of flora that have flowed in and out of this area through geologic time.

As a result, both the forest and shrub communities are diverse. Ponderosa pine, lodgepole pine, Douglas-fir, white fir and grand fir dominate the lower elevations. Open, parklike forests of subalpine fir, Engelmann spruce, limber pine, western white pine, whitebark pine and quaking aspen are characteristic of higher elevations. Rocky Mountain juniper is a common tree at hot, dry lower elevations near the Rockies, while western juniper is more common nearer the Cascades.

Many shrubs found here are of the same genera as those found in the Pacific and Sierran forests, but they are different species. One good example is Rocky Mountain maple, which largely replaces vine maple as a dominant understory shrub in Rocky Mountain forests. Alders, willows, cherries, serviceberries, elderberries, honeysuckles, huckleberries, currants, gooseberries, roses and snowberries are additional examples. Boxwoods and buffaloberries are more common here than in other Northwest forests.

Shrub communities and forest types

How shrub communities interact with these forest types depends on many factors. Perhaps the most important concept is that shrubs (as do other plants) grow where their ecological needs are met by the environment in which they find themselves, and where they can compete with other species that prefer a similar environment.

Some shrubs have specific requirements. Others can tolerate a much wider set of conditions. Therefore, some shrubs seem to move together with other members of their dominant flora, while others seem to move independently. The diversity of trees and shrubs is likely to be highest when environments conducive to species from all three major floras converge.

With increasing experience in the field, you'll begin to anticipate what shrubs will likely be found with others, and you'll begin to enjoy this additional challenge of understanding forest ecology.

Changes in elevation have helped create a diverse mix of species in forests east of the Cascades.

Shrubs grow where their ecological needs are met by the environment, and where they can compete with other species that prefer a similar environment.

The key to successful identification

Fortunately, you don't need to remember every plant or all characteristics of every plant. Keys help you make the most important distinctions. Keys come in all shapes and sizes. Some are based on pictures, while others use words. Some cover only trees, while others cover only wildflowers. Some are simple to use, while others are more difficult.

Dichotomous keys (like those used in this book) divide plants into two groups: those that have a particular characteristic and those that don't. If any group of plants is split often enough, eventually there will be only one type of plant left. If the key is accurate, and if you've made good decisions along the way, you'll have correctly identified the plant.

Using a key is like following the branches of a tree. Each additional branch gets smaller and smaller until you reach a single branch tip. The trunk represents all species described in a key, and each branch tip represents a single species.

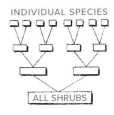

Using a key is like following the branches of a tree. Each additional branch gets smaller and smaller until you reach a single branch tip.

No matter how good the key, using it takes practice. Shrubs are often more difficult to key than trees for several reasons. There are more shrubs than there are trees, and shrubs' leaf characteristics are often more variable. For example, it's not uncommon for leaf size to vary dramatically depending on whether the shrub is growing in sun or shade, or for leaf shape to vary depending on whether the leaves are on young or old branches. And it's common for leaf margins to vary from smooth to serrated or even lobed, sometimes on the same plant. It's important to look at as many samples as you can and "average" the results before making a decision.

This book contains a single key for shrubs (beginning on page 26). Each step in the key consists of two descriptive statements. Read each statement, and decide which one best describes the plant you're trying to identify. Then follow the directions at the end of that statement, and each subsequent statement, until you arrive at a plant name.

I've tried to make the key simple to use, but that doesn't mean it's always simple to key shrubs. Judgment is often required, and judgment comes from practice and from making wrong decisions. For example, evergreen leaves are usually, but not always, thicker and more leathery than deciduous leaves. In this key, when I've noticed that challenge, I've often made it so you can key the plant by making either choice (even though one choice is correct and one is not because the leaves are either deciduous or they are not). Also, when leaves can be both lobed and unlobed (or serrated and not serrated) on the same plant, you can usually key correctly by making either choice. The species descriptions that follow the key contain the actual characteristics of each plant (although variability always exists in nature).

Because of these ambiguities, keying may be a bit difficult in the beginning. With practice, you'll fly through most specimens you encounter. The key to success is always practice.

Leaf composition

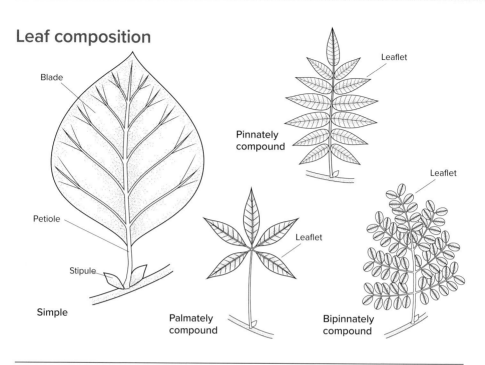

Blade

Petiole

Stipule

Simple

Pinnately compound

Leaflet

Palmately compound

Leaflet

Bipinnately compound

Leaflet

Leaf margins

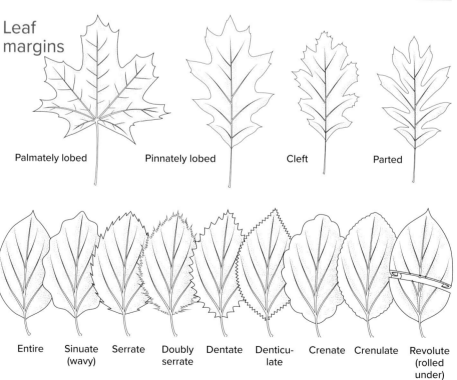

Palmately lobed

Pinnately lobed

Cleft

Parted

Entire

Sinuate (wavy)

Serrate

Doubly serrate

Dentate

Denticulate

Crenate

Crenulate

Revolute (rolled under)

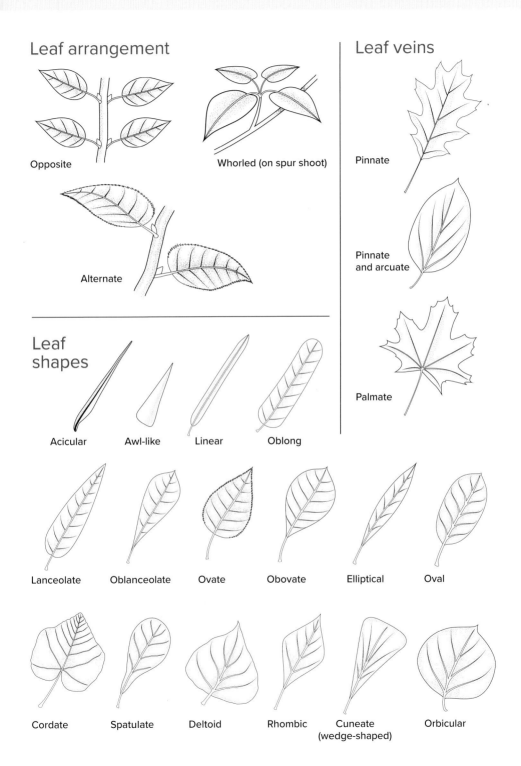

Leaf arrangement

Opposite

Whorled (on spur shoot)

Alternate

Leaf shapes

Acicular

Awl-like

Linear

Oblong

Lanceolate

Oblanceolate

Ovate

Obovate

Elliptical

Oval

Cordate

Spatulate

Deltoid

Rhombic

Cuneate (wedge-shaped)

Orbicular

Leaf veins

Pinnate

Pinnate and arcuate

Palmate

Leaf apexes

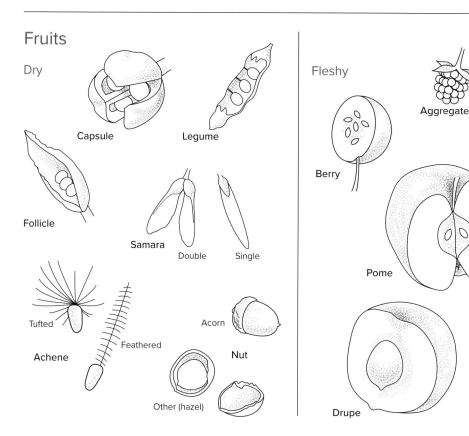

Acute Acumina Rounded Mucronate Obtuse Emarginate Truncate

Leaf bases

Acute Cuneate Obtuse Rounded Truncate Corda Inequilateral

Fruits

Dry

Capsule Legume

Follicle

Samara
Double Single

Tufted

Achene

Feathered

Acorn

Nut

Other (hazel)

Fleshy

Aggregate

Berry

Pome

Drupe

Flowers

Inflorescences (arrangements of individual flowers on a single or branched stalk)

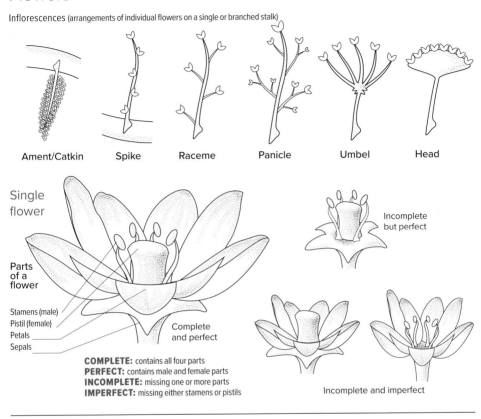

Ament/Catkin   Spike   Raceme   Panicle   Umbel   Head

Single flower

Incomplete but perfect

Parts of a flower

Stamens (male)
Pistil (female)
Petals
Sepals

Complete and perfect

COMPLETE: contains all four parts
PERFECT: contains male and female parts
INCOMPLETE: missing one or more parts
IMPERFECT: missing either stamens or pistils

Incomplete and imperfect

Twigs

Buds

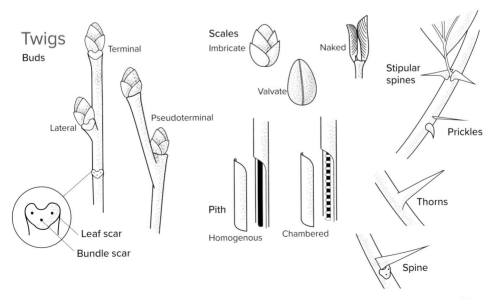

Terminal

Lateral

Pseudoterminal

Leaf scar

Bundle scar

Scales
Imbricate

Valvate

Naked

Pith

Homogenous   Chambered

Stipular spines

Prickles

Thorns

Spine

More terms to know

AMENT
Inflorescence in which the individual flowers are arranged along a central spike, are all the same sex, and do not have petals or stalks. Same as catkin.

ARCUATE
Curved toward the apex; typically refers to leaf veins.

ARMED
Covered in spines, prickles or thorns.

AWL-LIKE
Short, sharp and tapers to a fine point.

AXIL (AXILLARY)
Angle formed between the upper side of the petiole and the twig to which it's attached.

BERRYLIKE DRUPE
Unusual type of drupe containing multiple seeds (resembles a berry).

BIENNIAL
Plant that completes its life cycle over two years; produces vegetative growth the first year, fruits the second year and then dies.

BLOOM
White waxy or powdery covering on leaves, fruits or stems.

BRACT
Modified leaf often associated with flowers or inflorescences; often reduced in size; may be green or more colorful.

BROWSE
Refers to eating woody plants by nibbling and to the plants that are nibbled.

BURL
Woody, swollen, irregular tissue resembling a tumor; may be above or below the ground; important source of sprouts.

CALYX
Outermost whorl of the floral envelope; the collective set of sepals.

CANE
Another name for the main stem of blackberries and their relatives.

CLOSED STANDS/ FORESTS
Tree crowns touch (or nearly so), changing the quantity and quality of light in the understory.

CATKIN
Same as ament.

COMPLETE
A complete flower contains all four parts: pistils, stamens, sepals and petals.

COMPOUND
Leaf with multiple blades (leaflets) per petiole; may be pinnately or palmately compound.

COROLLA
Innermost whorl of the floral envelope; the collective set of petals.

CUTICLE
Waxy, waterproof layer covering most leaves and young stems.

DECIDUOUS
Falls off at the end of one growing season. Describes leaves that live only one season, and plants that lose all of their leaves at the end of one growing season.

DECOCTION
Refers to concentrating liquid by boiling, and to the resulting extract.

DICHOTOMOUS
Divided into two parts; forked.

DIOECIOUS
Male (staminate) and female (pistillate) flowers borne on separate plants.

DISTURBANCE
Alteration of an existing site by causes such as fire, wind or human activity.

DORMANT
Inactive; resting.

DORSAL
On the back side.

DRUPELET
Small drupe—a fleshy fruit containing a single hard seed. Blackberries are composed of multiple drupelets.

DUFF	Partially decomposed organic layer on the forest floor.
EARLY SUCCESSION	Initial stage of succession; often follows a substantial disturbance. Colonizing plants commonly face full sun and bare mineral soil; some plants may resprout from the previous forest.
EVERGREEN	Retains most leaves through more than one growing season. Evergreen plants are always covered in leaves; the leaves themselves are persistent.
EXFOLIATE (EXFOLIATING)	Peeling off in layers or flakes; commonly associated with bark.
FORAGE	Refers to obtaining food by browsing or grazing, and to the food obtained.
FRUIT	Ripened ovary of a plant; the seed-bearing organ.
GERMINATION	Period when seeds begin to grow — when radicle and cotyledons emerge from the seed.
GLABROUS	Smooth; no hairs.
GLANDS (GLANDULAR)	Plant organs that produce secretions; may be raised or sunken. Cherries and their relatives commonly have prominent glands on their petioles.
GLAUCOUS	Covered in bloom.
HYBRIDIZE (HYBRIDIZATION)	Reproduce across typical genetic boundaries (such as between members of different species).
IMBRICATE	Overlapping, like fish scales or roof shingles; often refers to bud scales.
IMPERFECT	An imperfect flower lacks either pistils or stamens; it may or may not have petals or sepals.
INCOMPLETE	An incomplete flower lacks one or more of the four parts: pistils, stamens, sepals or petals.
INFLORESCENCE	Arrangement of individual flowers in a particular, repeatable pattern (for example, ament, raceme, head).
INFUSION	Refers to steeping in hot liquid without boiling, and to the resulting product.
INNER BARK	Inner portion of the bark containing the cortex and phloem, which transports food within the tree; generally not protective like outer bark.
INVASIVE	Plants and plant populations that rapidly expand into a new area, especially where they are not native.
LATE SUCCESSION	Stage of succession eventually resulting from minimal disturbance over time; often characterized by mature trees, closed canopies and low light in the understory.
LATERAL	On the side (lateral buds, for example).
LAYER (LAYERING)	In this context, refers to buried branches that develop roots and aerial shoots, forming a clone of the "parent" plant.
LEAFLET	One leafy segment of a compound leaf.
LENTICEL	Raised pore on a stem that allows gas exchange between the atmosphere and plant.

LOW-SEVERITY FIRE Fire of low to modest heat and flame heights; burns some organic matter but not to mineral soil; typically affects understory but not mature trees with thick bark.

MAT-FORMING Grows in a low, dense form resembling a mat.

MISTLETOE Semiparasitic plant that commonly infects woody plants.

MONOECIOUS Male (staminate) and female (pistillate) flowers borne on the same plant in separate flowers.

NAKED BUD Bud lacks protective scales.

NECTAR Sugary liquid produced by plants to attract pollinators.

NETTED Veins that join together in a networked, or lacy, pattern.

NITROGEN-FIXING/ FIXER Refers to converting atmospheric nitrogen into forms plants can use, and to plants which contain bacteria that carry out this process.

NODE Place where a leaf arises from a stem.

OPEN STANDS/FORESTS Trees are widely spaced; light is generally not limiting to understory development.

PALATABILITY Acceptability of a particular plant for eating by a herbivore.

PENDULOUS Hangs down, like a pendant.

PERFECT A perfect flower has both pistils and stamens; it may or may not have sepals or petals.

PERSISTENT Remains attached, often longer than one growing season. Persistent leaves live longer than one growing season; plants with persistent leaves are commonly called evergreens.

PETAL One segment of the corolla; often scented and brightly colored.

PETIOLATE Has a petiole (leaf stalk).

PIONEER SPECIES Plant capable of invading disturbed sites, often facing bare ground, full sun and high temperatures.

PISTIL (PISTILLATE) Seed-bearing (female) organ of a flower. Pistillate means having pistils but no stamens.

PITH Central core of a twig, branch or stem; different species have piths of different sizes, colors, and textures.

POLLINATION (POLLINATORS) The process of a plant receiving pollen on its stigma. Pollinators (such as bees or butterflies) carry pollen from one plant to another.

PRICKLE Sharp-pointed projection arising from the bark or epidermis of a plant; may be straight or hooked; often break off easily. Compare with spine and thorn.

PROSTRATE Lying flat, or nearly so.

PUBESCENT (PUBESCENCE) Covered in hairs (pubescence); pubescence comes in many shapes, sizes and densities.

RACHIS Main stalk on which leaflets are borne on a compound leaf. In a pinnately compound leaf, the rachis extends from the bottom leaflet to the top leaflet.

RECEPTACLE End of the flower stalk that bears the main flower parts. Same as torus.

RESIN (PITCH) Sticky, aromatic substance produced by some plants (especially conifers) to help protect them against damage from insects, diseases and wounds. Not watery like sap.

RHIZOME	Underground stem capable of producing buds, leaves, and roots. Results in clones. Resembles roots, but does not play the same role in absorbing nutrients and water.
SAP	Watery liquid that carries nutrients and sugars throughout a plant. Differs from resin, which is much stickier and plays only a protective role.
SEMIPERSISTENT	Barely persistent (old leaves die as new leaves are added, for example), or persistent under some conditions but not others.
SEPAL	One segment of the calyx; usually green.
SERPENTINE SOIL	High in magnesium and heavy metals; low in other essential nutrients; often green; inhibits growth of many plants.
SESSILE	No stalk or petiole.
SIMPLE	Leaf with only one blade per petiole.
SPINE	Sharp-pointed modified leaf. In cacti, all leaves have been reduced to spines; gorse has some leaves but mostly spines. Compare with thorn and prickle.
SPROUT (SPROUTING)	Refers to a new shoot arising from the trunk, branch, root collar, roots, burls or rhizomes of a plant, and to the act of producing such a shoot.
SPUR SHOOT	Lateral branch that barely elongates each year, resulting in leaves that appear whorled because they are so close together. Spur shoots often bear clusters of fruit.
STAMEN (STAMINATE)	Pollen-bearing (male) organ of a flower. Staminate means having stamens but no pistils.
TERMINAL	At the end of a branch, stem or leaf.
THORN	Short, stiff, sharp-pointed modified branch; some have lateral buds and leaves. Woody and tough to break compared with spines and prickles.
TOOTHED	Has small teeth, usually on the edges of leaves. Often used when not wanting to specify a particular kind of tooth (such as serrate, crenate, dentate, etc.).
TORUS	Synonym for receptacle.
TRIFOLIATE	Leaf divided into three leaflets. Commonly used when it's difficult to tell if a compound leaf is pinnately or palmately compound.
UNARMED	No spines, prickles or thorns.
UNISEXUAL	Has only male or female organs in a single flower or inflorescence.
VALVATE	Two parts meet at the edges without overlapping, like a clamshell; often refers to bud scales.
VEINS	Bundles of vascular tissue in leaves (or elsewhere). Veins contain xylem and phloem for moving liquids throughout a plant.

Keying shrubs and vines

This key helps identify many shrubs and vines native or naturalized to Pacific Northwest forests. Using a series of choices, it will guide you to the genus level of the plant in question. Once the genus is identified, turn to the page or pages indicated and review the species in that genus. Then, make your best choice.

If you can't find the right match, return to the start, or to the place in the key where you were uncertain of which choice to make. When first learning to key, it may help to jot down the steps you've chosen, marking anywhere you're uncertain. It will shorten the process for you.

Plants are not always easy to key — and keys are imperfect. Leaves on the same plant sometimes vary dramatically. For example, they can vary by position on the plant, through the season or by the environment in which they are growing. Different species within the same genus can also have different characteristics. This key tries to account for this variability by making it possible to reach the same genus by following different paths. Approach plant identification like a detective searching for clues — and enjoy the process.

▶ **Read each statement of the couplet. Pick the one that best describes the specimen you're examining. Then follow the path indicated — either to a page, or onward toward another step. The sample below provides a graphic representation of how the key is designed.**

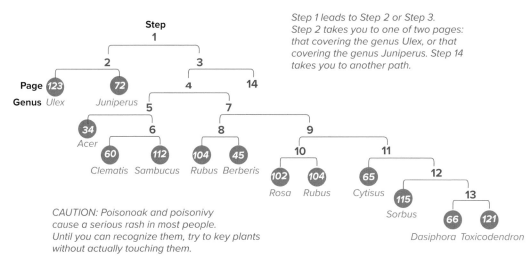

Step 1 leads to Step 2 or Step 3. Step 2 takes you to one of two pages: that covering the genus Ulex, or that covering the genus Juniperus. Step 14 takes you to another path.

CAUTION: Poisonoak and poisonivy cause a serious rash in most people. Until you can recognize them, try to key plants without actually touching them.

Steps		Genus	Go to
1	1a. Entire leaf needlelike or spiny (no broad leaf blade); sharp to the touch.		**STEP 2**
	1b. Leaves not as above; normal (wider) leaf blades. If blades are narrow, they are not spiny.		**STEP 3**
2	2a. Most leaves reduced to distinct, sharp spines (like sewing needles).	*Ulex* gorse	→ p. 123
	2b. Low-growing evergreen conifer. Leaves needlelike or awl-like; ternate (arranged in threes).	*Juniperus* juniper	→ p. 72

Steps		Genus	Go to
3	3a. All leaves simple.		**STEP 14**
	3b. All or most leaves compound (one species has both simple and trifoliate leaves on same plant).		**STEP 4**
4	4a. Leaves opposite (look at petiole of leaf, not leaflets).		**STEP 5**
	4b. Leaves alternate (look at petiole of leaf, not leaflets); may appear whorled.		**STEP 7**
5	5a. Leaves divided into three leaflets (some leaves simple).	*Acer* maple	**→ p. 34**
	5b. Leaves typically have five or more leaflets.		**STEP 6**
6	6a. Grows as trailing or climbing vine.	*Clematis* clematis	**→ p. 60**
	6b. Grows as upright shrub or small tree.	*Sambucus* elderberry	**→ p. 112**
7	7a. Leaves persistent (plant is evergreen). Leaves thick and leathery. Old leaves present with current year's leaves; old leaves may be different from current year's leaves in size or damage.		**STEP 8**
	7b. Leaves deciduous or appear deciduous (young leaves on evergreen plants sometimes appear deciduous, even when they are not).		**STEP 9**
8	8a. Stems and undersides of leaves armed with spines or prickles.	*Rubus* blackberry/raspberry	**→ p. 104**
	8b. Stems and undersides of leaves not armed with spines or prickles; leaflet margins spine-tipped.	*Berberis* Oregon-grape	**→ p. 45**
9	9a. Stems and leaves have spines or prickles.		**STEP 10**
	9b. Stems and leaves do not have spines or prickles.		**STEP 11**
10	10a. Leaves clearly pinnately compound with five or seven leaflets (sometimes more); prominent stipules. Showy, white to pink roses; fruits are rose hips.	*Rosa* rose	**→ p. 102**
	10b. Leaves pinnately or palmately compound with three or five leaflets; no stipules. Solitary flowers; aggregate fruits (like raspberries).	*Rubus* blackberry/raspberry	**→ p. 104**
11	11a. Simple and trifoliate leaves on same branch. Bright green, ribbed twigs. Bright yellow flowers; fruits are green or brown pods.	*Cytisus* Scotch broom	**→ p. 65**
	11b. One or more characteristics not as above.		**STEP 12**
12	12a. Typically seven to 13 leaflets arranged in a clear pinnate fashion.	*Sorbus* mountain-ash	**→ p. 115**
	12b. Leaflets not as above.		**STEP 13**
13	13a. Usually three to nine leaflets, each typically less than 1" long; arrangement may appear palmate but is actually pinnate.	*Dasiphora* shrubby cinquefoil	**→ p. 66**
	13b. Usually three leaflets (sometimes five); pinnate; irregularly lobed but never serrated. TOXIC when touched.	*Toxicodendron* poisonoak/poisonivy	**→ p. 121**
14	14a. Leaves, twigs, and spur shoots (if present) are opposite.		**STEP 15**
	14b. Leaves, twigs, and spur shoots (if present) are alternate.		**STEP 27**

Steps		Genus	Go to
15	15a. Leaves palmately lobed; three to 13 lobes.		**STEP 16**
	15b. Leaves not palmately lobed.		**STEP 17**
16	16a. Leaves have three to 13 lobes. Flowers small and green/yellow or red/white; fruits are double samaras.	*Acer* maple	**→ p. 34**
	16b. Leaves have only three lobes; coarse teeth (pointed or rounded). Flowers small, white, and clustered; fruits are bright red berries.	*Viburnum* viburnum	**→ p. 134**
17	17a. Leaves deciduous; generally thin and with less waxy cuticles (one species has thick leaves with brown dots on undersides of leaves and twigs).		**STEP 18**
	17b. Leaves persistent; thick and leathery. Old leaves may be different from current year's leaves in size or damage.		**STEP 24**
18	18a. Growth form is a climbing, twisting vine.	*Lonicera* honeysuckle	**→ p. 73**
	18b. Growth form not as above.		**STEP 19**
19	19a. All leaf margins toothed (may be lobed or unlobed).		**STEP 20**
	19b. Leaf margins not toothed. Most are entire, but one genus may have entire and lobed leaves on the same plant.		**STEP 21**
20	20a. Leaves elliptical to broadly ovate; sparse, glandular teeth. Large, white flowers; dry fruits.	*Philadelphus* mockorange	**→ p. 83**
	20b. Leaves broadly ovate to nearly round; regularly spaced coarse teeth. Small, white flowers in clusters; fruits are purple-black drupes.	*Viburnum* viburnum	**→ p. 134**
21	21a. Leaves thick and tough; appear persistent but are not; brown, raised dots on undersides of leaves; buds resemble praying hands.	*Shepherdia* buffaloberry	**→ p. 114**
	21b. Leaves thin; not thick.		**STEP 22**
22	22a. Leaves unlobed and often pinnately lobed on same plant. Small, pink-white flowers; white berries.	*Symphoricarpos* snowberry	**→ p. 119**
	22b. Leaves and fruits not as above.		**STEP 23**
23	23a. Leaf veins arcuate and parallel. When torn across midrib, leaf veins have distinct threads. Twigs red with clasping buds. Numerous tiny, white flowers in flat clusters; fruits are white to gray drupes.	*Cornus* dogwood	**→ p. 61**
	23b. Leaf veins arcuate but less tightly parallel than above; small veins distinctly netted. When torn, veins do not have threads. Flowers and fruits (berries) paired and surrounded by an involucre.	*Lonicera* honeysuckle	**→ p. 73**
24	24a. Leaf margins distinctly toothed.		**STEP 25**
	24b. Leaf margins entire or with very small teeth near apex.		**STEP 26**
25	25a. Plant hugs the ground like a dense mat. Leaf margins spiny.	*Ceanothus* ceanothus	**→ p. 49**
	25b. Plant grows upright. Leaf margins serrated but not spiny.	*Paxistima*/boxwood	**→ p. 82**
26	26a. Leaves 1 inch long or less; petiole very short; margins entire or with several small teeth near apex; many leaves on spur shoots.	*Ceanothus* ceanothus	**→ p. 49**
	26b. Most leaves substantially longer than 1 inch; petiole up to ½ inch long; margins entire.	*Garrya* silktassel	**→ p. 68**

Steps		Genus	Go to
27	27a. Leaves persistent; usually thick, leathery, and/or waxy. Leaves from different years are often different sizes and have different degrees of damage.		**STEP 28**
	27b. Leaves deciduous; thinner with less wax and thinner cuticles; size may vary on same plant. Most leaves have similar textures and types of damage.		**STEP 44**
28	28a. Only apex is lobed (not lateral margins); usually three distinct lobes; narrowly wedge-shaped; gray-green and pubescent on both surfaces.	*Artemisia* sagebrush	→ **p. 43**
	28b. One or more characteristics not as above.		**STEP 29**
29	29a. Stems armed with sharp thorns.	*Ceanothus* ceanothus	→ **p. 49**
	29b. Stems not armed with spines, thorns, or prickles.		**STEP 30**
30	30a. Leaf margins entire; no teeth.		**STEP 31**
	30b. Leaf margins toothed; teeth may be fine or coarse (one species has minute teeth that are often easier to feel than see).		**STEP 37**
31	31a. Leaves golden underneath; fruit a spiny bur.	*Chrysolepis* chinquapin	→ **p. 59**
	31b. Leaves and fruit not as above.		**STEP 32**
32	32a. Leaves elliptical to oval; prominently penniveined; veins raised above lower surface and gently arch toward apex; rusty hairs on petiole and midrib.	*Rhamnus* buckthorn	→ **p. 89**
	32b. Leaves not as above.		**STEP 33**
33	33a. Leaves generally 3–6 inches long; clustered near branch tips; margins slightly revolute; sometimes rusty below.	*Rhododendron* rhododendron/azalea	→ **p. 91**
	33b. Leaves generally 2 inches long or less.		**STEP 34**
34	34a. Mature plants seldom more than 18 inches tall; may be prostrate or mat-forming.		**STEP 35**
	34b. Mature plants clearly grow upright (not prostrate); commonly many feet tall.		**STEP 36**
35	35a. Undersides of leaves have sparse, minute, stiff hairs (may appear as dots); apex notched; margins revolute with indistinct serrations. Fruits are bright red berries.	*Vaccinium* blueberry/huckleberry	→ **p. 124**
	35b. Undersides of leaves do not have hairs; petioles sometimes hairy. Bark orange-red-brown and exfoliating. Fruits are berrylike drupes (multiple seeds).	*Arctostaphylos* manzanita	→ **p. 39**
36	36a. Leaves narrowly elliptical with revolute margins; commonly cupped around midrib; mostly clustered on spur shoots. Bark not exfoliating but may be scaly.	*Cercocarpus* mountain-mahogany	→ **p. 57**
	36b. Leaves elliptical to ovate; not revolute; not clustered on spur shoots. Bark is red-brown and clearly exfoliating.	*Arctostaphylos* manzanita	→ **p. 39**
37	37a. Many leaves borne on spur shoots; teeth concentrated above midpoint but regularly spaced.	*Cercocarpus* mountain-mahogany	→ **p. 57**
	37b. One or more characteristics not as above.		**STEP 38**

Steps		Genus	Go to
38	38a. Leaves obovate to oblanceolate; several coarse teeth along margins (sometimes entire). Grows upright or prostrate.	*Baccharis* coyotebrush	→ **p. 44**
	38b. Not as above.		**STEP 39**
39	39a. Leaves have three main veins from base.	*Ceanothus* ceanothus	→ **p. 49**
	39b. Leaves have one prominent midvein; lateral veins variable.		**STEP 40**
40	40a. Leaf margins indistinctly serrated and slightly revolute; apex often notched; tiny, sparse hairs on undersides of leaves turn black with age (use a hand lens to see).	*Vaccinium* blueberry/huckleberry	→ **p. 124**
	40b. Leaf margins distinctly serrated; apex not notched.		**STEP 41**
41	41a. Leaves ovate.		**STEP 42**
	41b. Leaves not ovate.		**STEP 43**
42	42a. Leaves less than 1½ inches long; folded up around midrib.	*Vaccinium* blueberry/huckleberry	→ **p. 124**
	42b. Leaves 2–4 inches long; primary lateral veins arcuate; smaller veins netted.	*Gaultheria* salal	→ **p. 70**
43	43a. Leaves oval to elliptical but not obovate; usually 2–4 inches long; prominently penniveined; veins often arch toward apex. Fruits are single-seeded drupes.	*Rhamnus* buckthorn	→ **p. 89**
	43b. Leaves narrowly elliptical to oblanceolate; 2–4 inches long; teeth regular but fewer toward base; teeth pointed or rounded; undersides have numerous white and/or black dots.	*Myrica* bayberry	→ **p. 79**
44	44a. Leaves, stems, and/or branches armed with spines, thorns or prickles.		**STEP 45**
	44b. Leaves, stems, and/or branches not armed.		**STEP 49**
45	45a. Branches armed with distinct, woody thorns or sharp-pointed branches; no spines/prickles on leaves; leaves not palmately lobed.		**STEP 46**
	45b. Stems, branches, and often leaves armed with spines and prickles; leaves palmately lobed.		**STEP 48**
46	46a. Woody thorns smooth; do not contain buds or small leaves.	*Crataegus* hawthorn	→ **p. 63**
	46b. Woody thorns are sharpened spur shoots; often contain buds and small leaves.		**STEP 47**
47	47a. Leaves singly serrated or serrated and lobed (on same plant); no glands on petiole or leaf base. Fruits are small pomes.	*Malus* crabapple	→ **p. 77**
	47b. Leaves serrated but never lobed and serrated; commonly have glands on petiole or leaf base. Fruits are drupes.	*Prunus* cherry/plum	→ **p. 85**
48	48a. Leaves generally less than 3 inches in diameter.	*Ribes* currant/gooseberry	→ **p. 94**
	48b. Leaves generally more than 5 inches in diameter.	*Oplopanax* devilsclub	→ **p. 81**
49	49a. Leaf margins totally entire (may be wavy or wrinkled).		**STEP 50**
	49b. Leaf margins lobed or toothed (may be partially or wholly toothed).		**STEP 57**

Steps		Genus	Go to
50	50a. Leaves linear; very narrow; similar to blades of grass.	*Ericameria* rabbitbrush	→ p. 67
	50b. Leaves not linear or very narrow.		STEP 51
51	51a. Leaves typically have three prominent veins from base (look beneath); 1–3 inches long; oblong to ovate; petiole typically ½" long.	*Ceanothus* ceanothus	→ p. 49
	51b. Leaves not as above.		STEP 52
52	52a. Most leaves have stipules; entire or with rounded teeth. Flowers are catkins (aments); fruits are cottony puffs that emerge from capsules.	*Salix* willow	→ p. 110
	52b. Leaves do not have stipules.		STEP 53
53	53a. Most leaves clustered near ends of stems; margins often wavy or wrinkled; not prominently penniveined. Large, trumpet-shaped flowers; fruits are capsules.	*Rhododendron* rhododendron/azalea	→ p. 91
	53b. Leaves, flowers, and fruits not as above.		STEP 54
54	54a. Leaves 2 to 5 inches long; elliptical to oblong; resemble rabbit ears; smell like cucumber. Twigs have orange lenticels and chambered pith.	*Oemleria* Indian-plum	p. 80 →
	54b. Leaves and twigs not as above.		STEP 55
55	55a. Leaves prominently penniveined; veins parallel but may arch toward apex; veins on undersides of leaves distinctly raised; fine pubescence on petioles and veins. Small, yellow-green flowers; fruits are purple to brown drupes.	*Rhamnus* buckthorn	→ p. 89
	55b. Veins not as above.		STEP 56
56	56a. Leaves usually less than 2 inches long; elliptical to oval; petioles short. Twigs thin and often bright green or red. Small, urn-shaped flowers; fruits are berries.	*Vaccinium* blueberry/huckleberry	→ p. 124
	56b. Leaves highly variable in size and shape. Typically several times longer than wide; typically 2–10 inches long; elliptical to lanceolate to ovate or obovate; margins entire or toothed. Undersides may be similar in color to top or range from brown to white; surfaces smooth to highly pubescent; with or without stipules. Twigs often supple and yellow-green to red. Flowers are catkins (aments); fruits are cottony puffs with tiny seeds that emerge from capsules. Typically robust shrubs to small trees on moist sites.	*Salix* willow	→ p. 110
57	57a. Only apex is lobed (three to five distinct lobes); lateral margins entire; typically less than 1" long and wedge-shaped.	*Purshia* bitterbrush	→ p. 88
	57b. Not as above; substantial portion of margins toothed or lobed.		STEP 58
58	58a. Leaves palmately lobed.		STEP 59
	58b. Leaves pinnately lobed or not lobed at all.		STEP 61
59	59a. Leaves typically five-lobed and 3–10 inches wide (most commonly large); generally as wide as they are long; both surfaces covered in dense, velvety hairs. Large, white flowers; fruits are red raspberries.	*Rubus* blackberry/raspberry	p. 104
	59b. Leaves typically have three to seven lobes; ½–10 inches wide; may have pubescence, but not thick and velvety; many species (not all) have sticky or smelly leaves.		STEP 60

Steps		Genus	Go to
60	60a. Bark exfoliates freely in long strips. Small, white flowers in upright, dome-shaped clusters; fruits are brown follicles in dome-shaped clusters. Leaves not sticky or aromatic.	*Physocarpus* ninebark	→ **p. 84**
	60b. Bark may stay tight or split and appear shreddy. Small, trumpet-shaped flowers; single, clustered, or in spikes; fruits are berries, often with glandular hairs. Leaves often sticky and/or smelly.	*Ribes* currant/gooseberry	→ **p. 94**
61	61a. Leaves doubly serrated or lobed and serrated (often subtle difference).		**STEP 62**
	61b. Leaves singly serrated or toothed (never doubly serrated or lobed); some margins entire, or at least appear entire until close inspection.		**STEP 65**
62	62a. Leaves irregularly lobed with one to several lobes per leaf; some leaves serrated but not lobed on same stem; spur shoots common.	*Malus* crabapple	→ **p. 77**
	62b. Leaves doubly serrated or lobed with numerous, regularly spaced lobes.		**STEP 63**
63	63a. Leaves broadly ovate to nearly round; sharply and doubly serrated; leaves, petioles, and young twigs very pubescent; young twigs zigzag.	*Corylus* hazel	→ **p. 62**
	63b. Leaves and especially twigs not as above.		**STEP 64**
64	64a. Leaves 1–3 inches long; coarsely toothed, doubly toothed, or lobed and toothed. Tiny, white flowers in large, terminal clusters; fruits are brown follicles in large, terminal clusters.	*Holodiscus* oceanspray	→ **p. 71**
	64b. Leaves 2–6 inches long; prominently penniveined. Flowers are catkins; fruits are persistent, woody cones. Young twigs typically triangular. Grows as large shrub or small tree.	*Alnus* alder	→ **p. 36**
65	65a. Leaves have asymmetrical base and shape; apex acuminate (often sickle-shaped); stiff, sandpaper-like hairs; veins distinctly netted.	*Celtis* hackberry	→ **p. 56**
	65b. One or more characteristics not as above.		**STEP 66**
66	66a. Leaves have three prominent veins from base (look underneath); teeth rounded rather than sharp.	*Ceanothus* ceanothus	→ **p. 49**
	66b. Leaves not as above.		**STEP 67**
67	67a. Most leaves have two to four distinct glands (green, yellow-green, or red) on base and/or petiole (sometimes small or absent); some have paired stipules.	*Prunus* cherry, plum	→ **p. 85**
	67b. Leaves do not have distinct glands.		**STEP 68**
68	68a. Leaves ovate; 2–5 inches long; margin distinctly serrated or doubly serrated for most of its length; teeth pointed or rounded. Flowers are catkins; fruits are persistent, woody cones. Young twigs typically triangular.	*Alnus* alder	→ **p. 36**
	68b. Leaves, flowers, fruits, and twigs not as above.		**STEP 69**
69	69a. Leaves 1–2 inches long; oval to nearly round; prominently penniveined; toothed near apex but not near base; teeth near apex point toward apex. Flower petals white and straplike; fruits are blue pomes.	*Amelanchier* serviceberry	→ **p. 38**
	69b. Leaves, flowers, and fruits not as above.		**STEP 70**

Steps		Genus	Go to
70	70a. Leaves ½–2 inches long; ovate, obovate, or nearly round; coarse teeth along most of margin; spur shoots common. Flowers are catkins; fruits are papery cones.	*Betula* birch	→ **p. 48**
	70b. One or more characteristics not as above.		**STEP 71**
71	71a. Leaves 1–3 inches long; petiole very short; most leaves have coarse serrations above midpoint, but some are mostly serrated; oblong to elliptical or ovate to obovate. Tiny, pink to red flowers in dense clusters; fruits are brown follicles in dense clusters.	*Spiraea* spirea	→ **p. 117**
	71b. One or more characteristics not as above.		**STEP 71**
72	72a. Prominently penniveined; veins very parallel; primary and lateral veins distinctly raised above lower leaf surface.	*Rhamnus* buckthorn	→ **p. 89**
	72b. Leaves not as above.		**STEP 73**
73	73a. Leaves often lobed and unlobed on same plant or branch; distinctly serrated; numerous spur shoots with whorled leaves. White, showy flowers; fruits are pomes.	*Malus* crabapple	→ **p. 77**
	73b. One or more characteristics not as above.		**STEP 74**
74	74a. Leaves have distinct stipules.	*Salix* willow	→ **p. 110**
	74b. Leaves do not have stipules.		**STEP 75**
75	75a. Leaves ⅜–2 inches long; elliptical, ovate, or obovate; finely toothed above midpoint or along entire margin. Urn-shaped flowers; fruits are berries.	*Vaccinium* blueberry/huckleberry	→ **p. 124**
	75b. One or more characteristics not as above.		**STEP 76**
76	76a. Leaves 1–3 inches long; elliptical to obovate; finely toothed with nippled tip at apex. Urn-shaped, orange/salmon flowers; fruits are dry capsules. Typically a spindly shrub.	*Menziesia* menziesia	→ **p. 78**
	76b. Leaves highly variable in size and shape. Typically several times longer than wide; typically 2–10 inches long; elliptical to lanceolate to ovate or obovate; margins entire or toothed. Undersides may be similar in color to top or range from brown to white; surfaces smooth to highly pubescent; with or without stipules. Twigs often supple and yellow-green to red. Flowers are catkins (aments); fruits are cottony puffs with tiny seeds that emerge from capsules. Typically robust shrubs to small trees on moist sites.	*Salix* willow	→ **p. 110**

Form: Erect shrub with multiple stems and crooked branches in a helter-skelter arrangement; 20–40 feet tall.

Leaves: Simple, opposite, deciduous. Palmately lobed and veined; five to nine (usually seven) shallow, toothed lobes; lobes fanlike; outline circular; commonly 2–5 inches in diameter but larger in shade. Green above; pale green below.

Flowers/fruit: Small flowers borne in short, terminal clusters; red sepals and white petals. Fruits are double samaras with wings nearly straight out from one another; each wing 1–2 inches long; bright red turning brown at maturity.

Twigs/bark: Twigs slender; smooth; round; typically green to red-brown. Lateral buds small and opposite; terminal buds paired and dichotomous. Bark thin, smooth and greenish regardless of age; often covered in moss and lichens.

Range/habitat: More common west of the Cascade crest than east of it. Grows in dense shade to full sun on a variety of moist soils. Pioneer species on cut and burned areas but also common in mature forests.

Notes: Grows dense and upright in sun but leggy and tangled in shade. Forms graceful arches in old-growth forests. Branches touching the ground often root, forming dense clones. In fall, among the most colorful plants in Pacific Northwest forests. Leaves turn yellow in shade and bright red in sun. Not commercially valuable except as a landscape plant. Indigenous people use its supple branches to tie logs and make nets and snowshoes and use its wood for utensils and firewood. Variable quality browse for mammals; birds and small mammals eat its seeds. In forests, reproduction by layering and sprouting is more common than by seed.

Names: Maple family, *Aceraceae*. *Acer* is the Latin name for maples; *circinatum* refers to round leaves. Called devilwood by Canadian trappers and octopus-of-the-woods by loggers.

Compare with: other maples, ninebark, currants.

Form: Erect shrub or small tree, commonly with multiple stems; 20–40 feet tall.

Leaves: Simple (but sometimes compound on the same plant), opposite, deciduous. Palmately lobed; typically three large and two small lobes; margins toothed to serrated; commonly 2–7 inches in diameter. Green above and below.

Flowers/fruit: Small, yellow or green flowers borne in short, terminal clusters of five to 10. Fruits are double samaras with wings close together (up to 80 degrees apart); each wing is about 1 inch long.

Twigs/bark: Twigs opposite; slender; smooth; round; bright red to red-brown. Buds small; dark red. Bark gray-brown; smooth when young; fissured with age.

Range/habitat: *A. glabrum* has the widest range of any western maple. Ranges from southeastern Alaska to the Mexican border and from the Pacific Coast to the east side of the Rockies; 1,000–10,000 feet depending on latitude. Numerous local varieties exist. Douglas maple is the most common variety west of the Cascade crest. Grows on dry to moist sites; riparian and upland; and in open and closed forests.

Notes: Spindly in closed stands but bushy with more light. Important browse for wildlife and livestock; intense browsing often limits size. Grouse eat its leaves and buds; many animals eat its seeds. Commonly used in streamside restoration. Early to late-successional species. Sensitive to fire but survives by sprouting. Some Indigenous people use its supple branches to make snowshoes and cradles and inner bark to make twine. Eriophyid mite outbreaks sometimes cause bright red blotches on leaves.

Names: Maple family, *Aceraceae*. *Acer* is the Latin name for maples; *glabrum* refers to smooth, hairless leaves; *douglasii* refers to Scottish botanist and plant explorer David Douglas.

Compare with: other maples, ninebark, currant.

Form: Thicket-forming shrub or small tree; 15–30 feet tall; stems 4–8 inches in diameter. Often crooked or leaning.

Leaves: Simple, alternate, deciduous. Ovate to oval; 2–6 inches long; margins doubly serrated, or shallowly lobed and serrated. Dull green on both sides; sometimes hairy below.

Flowers/fruit: Flowers borne in unisexual catkins (aments) on the same plant. Male catkins 1–4 inches long; slender and pendent; form in fall but remain unopened through winter; smaller female catkins occur above males. Fruits are small (½-inch-long), semiwoody cones; green turning brown; persist through winter. Seeds are tiny, winged nutlets.

Twigs/bark: Twigs slender; reddish and hairy when young; gray with age. Bark gray and smooth; scaly with age.

Range/habitat: The most widely distributed alder in western North America. Ranges from Alaska to New Mexico and from California to the eastern Rockies; 0–10,000 feet. *A. incana* is distributed across North America, Europe, and Asia, with multiple local subspecies. Our most common variety, thinleaf or mountain alder, is confined to western North America. Common along streams and rivers and on moist sites; often in disturbed areas but also shade tolerant.

Notes: Browsed by wildlife and domestic animals, but value varies. Often used in streamside restoration. Indigenous people make red dye from its inner bark and use the wood for smoking salmon. Fixes nitrogen. Prolific seed producer; also sprouts from base and branches.

Names: Birch family, *Betulaceae.* Taxonomy of speckled alder is currently in flux. *Alnus* is the Latin name for alders; *incana* means hairy, gray, or silver; *tenuifolia* refers to thin leaves. Thinleaf alder was formerly called *A. tenuifolia.*

Compare with: California hazel, other alders and birches.

Form: Thicket-forming shrub or small tree; 3–40 feet tall; stems to 10 inches in diameter. Often crooked or leaning.

Leaves: Simple, alternate, deciduous. Ovate to oval; 2–5 inches long; margins either singly or doubly serrated; often wavy. Green to yellow-green above; paler green and sticky below.

Flowers/fruit: Flowers borne in unisexual catkins (aments) on the same plant. Male catkins long, slender, and pendent; form in fall but open with leaves in spring; small, female catkins hang in long-stalked clusters above males. Fruits are small (½– to 1-inch long), semiwoody cones; green turning brown; persist through winter. Seeds are tiny, winged nutlets.

Twigs/bark: Twigs slender; orange-brown and sticky when young; gray and smooth with age; conspicuous lenticels. Buds slender and pointed with valvate scales; nearly sessile. Bark gray; thin; smooth with warty lenticels.

Range/habitat: *A. viridis* is widely distributed across the Northern Hemisphere, with several subspecies in North America. Sitka alder ranges from Alaska to northern California and into the Rockies and is common in Oregon and Washington. Grows on poorly drained sites from sea level to tree line depending on latitude. Common in avalanche tracks and glacial outwash plains.

Notes: Commonly invades disturbed sites because of its nitrogen-fixing ability and prolific seed production. Fast growing but short lived. Wood is used for fuel and smoking fish.

Names: Birch family, *Betulaceae*. Taxonomy is in flux. *Alnus* is the Latin name for alders; *viridis* means green; *sinuata* refers to wavy leaf margins. Sitka refers to its prominence near Sitka, Alaska. Related subspecies are called green, mountain, and Siberian alder.

Compare with: California hazel, other alders and birches.

Form: Erect shrub to 40 feet tall; stems 6–12 inches in diameter. Typically grows in clusters because of sprouting but may grow as a small tree.

Leaves: Simple, alternate, deciduous. Small (1–2 inches long); oval; prominently penniveined; veins extend to teeth; margins toothed near apex but entire near rounded base; petiole short.

Flowers/fruit: Flowers borne in short clusters; each flower has five long (up to 1-inch-long), white, straplike petals. Fruits are small (¼- to ½-inch), round, dark blue pomes; often covered in white bloom; often infected with orange fungus.

Twigs/bark: Twigs slender; smooth; red-brown when young; gray-brown with age. Buds about ½ inch long; red, imbricate scales with hairs along margins. Bark thin; light brown and tinged with red; smooth or shallowly fissured.

Range/habitat: Widely distributed across western North America and into eastern Canada. Occurs on moist, well-drained sites in sun or partial shade.

Notes: Deer and elk browse its twigs; birds and mammals enjoy the fruits. Indigenous people eat its fruits fresh and dried; use various parts as drops for eyes and ears, for treating colds, flu and fever, for improving appetite, and for birth control and laxatives; and use the branches for arrow shafts and digging sticks.

Names: Rose family, *Rosaceae*. *Amelanchier* may be a French name for a related plant; *alnifolia* refers to alder-like leaves. Other common names include Saskatoon serviceberry, western shadbush, western serviceberry and juneberry. Shadbush refers to flowering in early spring, when the shad run; juneberry refers to the time of fruit ripening. Saskatoon, Saskatchewan, is named after this plant.

Compare with: mountain-ash.

Form: Large, bushy evergreen shrub with stiff, gnarly branches; to 12 feet tall; stems to 5 inches in diameter.

Leaves: Simple, alternate, persistent. Small (1–2 inches long); generally elliptical to oval; margins entire; petiole short and hairy. Leathery; dull green or blue-green; hairy on both surfaces.

Flowers/fruit: Small, pink-white, urn-shaped flowers borne in small, terminal clusters. Fruits are small (¼- to ½-inch), round, smooth, red to coffee-colored, berrylike drupes that resemble tiny apples.

Twigs/bark: Young twigs gray and distinctly hairy; dark red-brown and smooth with age. Bark smooth and brown when young; flaky and dark red-brown with age.

Range/habitat: Occurs in full sun on well-drained, sandy or gravelly soils on the west side of the Cascades and Sierras from Washington through California; especially common in southwest Oregon. Colonizes sites after disturbance but also occurs in open forests. Does not tolerate dense shade.

Notes: Crooked branches and burls are made into novelties; very hard wood burns hot and bright. Its fruits are eaten by many animals but may cause constipation in humans; hummingbirds like the flowers; leaves and stems are not palatable to wildlife or livestock. Seeds require scarification by fire or animal digestion to break dormancy. Early to midsuccessional species.

Names: Heath family, *Ericaceae*. In Greek, *arctos* refers to bear and *staphyle* to bunches of grapes (in reference to fruits). Manzanita is Spanish for "little apple" and refers to fruits; hairy refers to hairs on leaves and twigs.

Compare with: other manzanitas and ceanothuses.

Form: Moderate-sized evergreen shrub with stiff, gnarly branches; 3–7 feet tall.

Leaves: Simple, alternate, persistent. Small (1–2 inches long); ovate to elliptical; margins entire. Leathery; green, shiny, and smooth on both surfaces. Often stand on edge during the heat of the day to reduce heat and water loss.

Flowers/fruit: Small, pink-white, urn-shaped flowers borne in small, terminal clusters. Fruits are small (¼-inch), round, smooth, red-brown to black, berrylike drupes that resemble tiny apples.

Twigs/bark: Bark smooth and brown on young stems; dark red-brown and exfoliating on older stems.

Range/habitat: Grows primarily east of the Cascades in Oregon but throughout much of California, Nevada and Arizona. Occurs in full sun on dry, well-drained sites from 2,500–6,000 feet and in open coniferous forests. Common on open lava flats and buttes with high sunlight and heat; also on burned sites. Very drought tolerant.

Notes: Provides good cover and preferred browse for mule deer. Its small, hard seeds can remain in the soil for decades before germinating. Also reproduces by branch layering and sometimes sprouts from underground burls. Leaves have low palatability, but animals eat its fruits and seeds. California alone has more than 50 manzanita species.

Names: Heath family, *Ericaceae*. In Greek, *arctos* refers to bear and *staphyle* to bunches of grapes (in reference to fruits); *patula* means spreading. Manzanita is Spanish for "little apple" and refers to fruits; green refers to leaf color. Also called green manzanita.

Compare with: other manzanitas and ceanothuses.

Form: Mat-forming evergreen shrub; seldom more than 1 foot tall.

Leaves: Simple, alternate, persistent. Small (½–1 inch long); elliptical to obovate; margins entire; tips rounded or slightly notched. Leathery; green and smooth on both surfaces, but young leaves may have soft pubescence.

Flowers/fruit: Small, pink to white, urn-shaped flowers borne in small, terminal clusters. Fruits are small (¼ inch in diameter), round, smooth, red, berrylike drupes that resemble tiny apples.

Twigs/bark: Twigs slender and trailing; frequently root at nodes; upright stems usually less than 1 foot tall. Bark smooth or scaly; dark red-brown; commonly flaky and exfoliating on older stems.

Range/habitat: Grows across the Northern Hemisphere at high latitudes and high elevations; the only manzanita that grows outside of North and Central America. Occurs on a variety of soils but does best in full sun or light shade from sea level to tree line. Common on sites with low productivity, acidic or granitic soils, and rapid drainage.

Notes: Many animals (including bears, deer, elk, bighorn sheep, moose and birds) eat its leaves and fruits. Humans eat the fruits, but many find them tasteless. Indigenous people smoke the leaves and use its fruits and leaves to cure many ailments, including kidney and bladder problems. Spreading growth form helps reduce erosion. Common ornamental. Reproduction is primarily vegetative.

Names: Heath family, *Ericaceae*. In Greek, *arctos* refers to bear and *staphyle* to bunches of grapes (in reference to fruits); *uva-ursi* refers to bears that eat its fruits. Kinnikinnick is an Algonquin word for a smoking mixture made from its leaves. Also called bearberry and mealberry.

Compare with: other low-growing manzanitas and ceanothuses.

Form: Moderate to large evergreen shrub with stiff, gnarly branches; 3–13 feet tall. Smooth, red branches often exposed.

Leaves: Simple, alternate, persistent. Small (1–2 inches long); ovate to nearly round; margins entire (sometimes slightly toothed). Leathery; both surfaces covered in dull, white bloom; sticky hairs in spring disappear with age. Typically stand on edge during the heat of the day to reduce heat and water loss.

Flowers/fruit: Small, pink-white, nearly conical flowers borne in small, terminal clusters (often abundant); sticky. Fruits are small (¼-inch), round, red-brown, berrylike drupes that resemble tiny apples; smooth or with sticky, glandular hairs.

Twigs/bark: Young twigs smooth or covered in fine hairs. Older bark exfoliates, leaving smooth, red-brown branches.

Range/habitat: Grows in Mediterranean climates of California and southwest Oregon; 500–5,000 feet. Common chaparral species. Found on sunny, dry slopes with shallow, rocky soils; also on serpentine soils.

Notes: Hybridizes with greenleaf manzanita. Poor browse value, but many animals eat its fruits. Fruits are sometimes made into jelly; Indigenous people eat and make cider from the berries. Seeds often remain in the soil for long periods until germinated by fire; also reproduces by layering and sprouting. Early successional species; often colonizes disturbed sites. Branch dieback, exfoliating bark, and leaves and twigs full of volatile oils and terpenes encourage fire. California alone has more than 50 manzanita species.

Names: Heath family, *Ericaceae*. In Greek, *arctos* refers to bear and *staphyle* to bunches of grapes (in reference to fruits); *viscida* means sticky. Manzanita is Spanish for "little apple" and refers to fruits. Also called sticky manzanita.

Compare with: other manzanitas and ceanothuses.

Form: Upright evergreen shrub; commonly 3–15 feet tall.

Leaves: Simple, alternate (but typically clustered at each node), persistent (some leaves are drought deciduous). Small (½–1 inch long); narrowly wedge-shaped with 3-lobed apex; sessile. Silvery-green and pubescent on both surfaces; strongly scented.

Flowers/fruit: Small, yellowish, tubular flowers borne in small heads on long, upright spikes. Fruits are small achenes; four- or five-sided or ribbed.

Twigs/bark: Twigs slender, silver-gray and pubescent when young; gray-brown with age. Bark gray-brown; shreddy; splits lengthwise.

Range/habitat: The most abundant shrub in the arid West. Ranges widely across the dry Intermountain West, from British Columbia to northern Baja California and from the Sierra-Cascades into the Dakotas and Nebraska. Typically grows at lower elevations but sometimes reaches tree line. Grows on open range and in open pine and juniper forests. Common invader of overgrazed grasslands.

Notes: Despite low palatability, its abundance makes it an important browse species for wild and domestic animals. State flower of Nevada. Tall, dense stands are indicative of fertile sites suitable for irrigated farming. Sensitive to fire; fire reduces its abundance.

Names: Sunflower family, *Asteraceae*. *Artemisia* commemorates Greek goddess Artemis, who is said to have benefitted from this plant; *tridentata* refers to three-toothed leaves. Several varieties exist and are called basin big sagebrush, mountain big sagebrush and Wyoming big sagebrush.

Compare with: bitterbrush, rabbitbrush, other sagebrushes.

Form: Evergreen shrub; prostrate or upright to 9 feet tall. May form dense mats on sand dunes.

Leaves: Simple, alternate, persistent. Small (½–2 inches long); obovate to oblanceolate (widest point above midpoint); margins range from entire to sparsely and coarsely toothed near apex; revolute; base wedge-shaped; apex acute to rounded; most leaves exhibit three primary veins (sometimes subtle). Thick and waxy; gray-green; glandular and often sticky.

Flowers/fruit: Small flowers borne in small, profuse, upright clusters; dioecious; female flowers white; male flowers yellow; blooms August through December. Fruits are tiny, windborne, tufted achenes (similar to thistles).

Twigs/bark: Young twigs green; grooved or ribbed; minutely pubescent; often sticky. Older twigs gray-brown; ribbed; roughened by leaf scars. Bark gray-brown; rough.

Range/habitat: Primarily coastal but grows west of the Cascades in Oregon and much of California; 0–1,500 feet. Common on sand dunes, coastal bluffs and open oak woodlands. Common member of coastal scrub communities in northern California.

Notes: Indigenous people use its straight shoots for arrow shafts and brew the leaves into tea as a general remedy. Prostrate form is useful for stabilizing sand dunes. Moderately fire tolerant; sprouts from roots and root crown; seeds prefer soil cleared by fire. Low browse value. Tolerates drought, browsing and poor soil. Characteristics of the two distinct forms intergrade.

Names: Sunflower family, *Asteraceae*. *Baccharis* is derived from Greek and refers to a plant with fragrant roots; *pilularis* means ball-shaped and refers to its flowers. Also called kidneywort baccharis, coyote bush and chaparral broom.

Compare with: evergreen huckleberry, some ceanothuses and coastal sages.

Form: Erect evergreen shrub; 3–12 feet tall. Commonly grows in dense clusters.

Leaves: Pinnately compound, alternate, persistent. Compound leaves 6–12 inches long; five to seven (rarely nine) broadly lanceolate leaflets, each 2–3 inches long; similar ornamental species often have seven to 11 leaflets. Leaflets dark glossy green above and pale green below; thick, waxy cuticles; sharp-spined teeth along margins. Lateral leaflets opposite and sessile; terminal leaflet has a petiole; individual leaflets have distinct midribs (similar to creeping Oregon-grape but unlike dwarf Oregon-grape).

Flowers/fruit: Small, bright yellow flowers borne in long, upright racemes. Fruits are small (³⁄₁₆-inch), dark blue berries; edible but sour.

Twigs/bark: Main stems largely unbranched; compound leaves commonly arise directly from main stems. Twigs green when young; gray-brown with age. Bark gray-brown; smooth or slightly rough; sometimes striped when mature.

Range/habitat: Occurs primarily, but not exclusively, on the west side of the Cascades. Grows on dry to moist, well-drained sites in sun or deep shade. Often indicates a warm, dry site. Tolerant of shade and understory conditions.

Notes: Occasional browse for deer and elk; birds and mammals eat its fruits. Fruits are excellent for jam and jelly; foliage is used in floral arrangements. Indigenous people use infusions and teas made from its bark as eyewash and to treat sore throats and stomachaches. They also make an important, bright yellow dye from broken roots.

Names: Barberry family, *Berberidaceae*. *Berberis* is a Latinized Arabic word; *aquifolium* refers to holly-like leaves. Tall refers to its height relative to other Oregon-grapes. Also called holly-grape and hollyleaved barberry, especially in the nursery trade. *Mahonia* is a common synonym for *Berberis*, especially in horticulture.

Compare with: other Oregon-grapes, American and introduced hollies.

Form: Low evergreen shrub; seldom more than 3 feet tall.

Leaves: Pinnately compound, alternate, persistent. Compound leaves 10–16 inches long; 11–21 broadly ovate to almost lanceolate leaflets, each 2–3 inches long. Leaflets dark glossy green above and paler below; thick, waxy cuticles; spined teeth along margins. Lateral leaflets opposite and sessile; terminal leaflet has a petiole; leaflets lack prominent midribs but have a distinctive, netlike pattern (other Oregon-grapes have prominent midribs).

Flowers/fruit: Small, bright yellow flowers borne in long, upright racemes. Fruits are small (³⁄₁₆-inch), dark blue berries; edible but sour.

Twigs/bark: Stems stout; numerous; upright. Main stem brown; compound leaves emerge directly from main stem; leaves cluster at terminal end. Numerous stiff bud scales persist at stem ends.

Range/habitat: Prefers moist, well-drained sites in sun or shade but can tolerate darker, wetter, and colder conditions than tall Oregon-grape. Common in moist Pacific Northwest forests.

Notes: Popular ornamental; florists use its foliage for greenery. Birds and mammals eat its fruits; deer browse the foliage, but it has low palatability. Reproduces by seed and rhizomes. Indigenous people use its berries to treat assorted liver, gall bladder and eye problems and make an important, bright yellow dye from broken roots.

Names: Barberry family, *Berberidaceae*. *Berberis* is a Latinized Arabic word; *nervosa* refers to nerve-like veins in leaves. Also called dull Oregon-grape, Cascade Oregon-grape, creeping mahonia, creeping hollygrape, and Cascade barberry. *Mahonia* is a common synonym for *Berberis*, especially in horticultur.

Compare with: other Oregon-grapes, American and introduced hollies.

Form: Creeping evergreen shrub; seldom more than 12 inches tall.

Leaves: Pinnately compound, alternate, persistent. Compound leaves 4–8 inches long; three to seven (usually five) broadly lanceolate leaflets (apex commonly rounded but may be pointed), each 2–3 inches long. Leaflets dull blue-green above and paler below; thick, waxy cuticles; spined teeth along margins. Lateral leaflets opposite and sessile; terminal leaflet has a petiole; leaflets have prominent midribs (similar to tall Oregon-grape).

Flowers/fruit: Small, bright yellow flowers borne in long, upright racemes. Fruits are small (³⁄₁₆-inch), dark blue berries borne in long, grapelike clusters; edible but sour.

Twigs/bark: Stems slender and mostly prostrate; short, upright stems often arise from underground rhizomes. Main stem brown; compound leaves emerge directly from main stem; leaves cluster at terminal end.

Range/habitat: The most common and widely distributed Oregon-grape in the West; most common Oregon-grape in eastern Oregon and Washington. Prefers hillsides and open pine forests from mid to high elevations. Tolerates low moisture, cold temperatures, and poor, rocky soils.

Notes: Leaves turn brilliant red in fall despite being evergreen (red leaves are replaced by new, green leaves the next spring). Reproduces by seed, layering and rhizomes growing just below the mineral soil surface. Pollinated by bees and butterflies. Indigenous people make an important, bright yellow dye from broken roots.

Names: Barberry family, *Berberidaceae*. *Berberis* is a Latinized Arabic word; *repens* refers to spreading growth form. Also called creeping mahonia, creeping hollygrape, mountain holly, creeping western barberry, and similar combinations. *Mahonia* is a common synonym for *Berberis*, especially in horticulture.

Compare with: other Oregon-grapes, American and introduced hollies.

Form: Erect shrub with many stems and branches; to 12 feet tall.

Leaves: Simple, alternate, deciduous. Small (½–1½ inches); broadly ovate to obovate to round; margins have rounded teeth; petiole short and reddish. Thicker than many deciduous leaves; dark green and smooth above, paler and glandular below.

Flowers/fruit: Flowers borne in unisexual catkins (aments) on the same plant. Male catkins form in fall, persist through winter, and hang in clusters; female catkins are solitary and upright. Fruits are papery strobiles (elongated cones) about ¾ inch long; fall apart at maturity. Seeds are tiny, winged nutlets.

Twigs/bark: Twigs slender; crooked; gray-brown to red-brown; very sticky resin dots when young, but resin hardens with age. Bark thin and smooth except for prominent, horizontal lenticels; gray-brown to red-brown; doesn't readily exfoliate.

Range/habitat: One of our most common and widely distributed birches. Ranges from Alaska into California and east across Canada into Greenland and New England; 1,300–11,000 feet. Usually grows near water (in mountain meadows and bogs, near springs and seeps); in the north, often grows in permafrost muskegs. Shade intolerant.

Notes: Grouse, quail and ptarmigans eat its buds; moose, caribou, deer, elk, mountain goats and grizzly bears browse its leaves and twigs. Hybridizes with other birches. Reproduces by windblown seed, layering and sprouting from the root crown and rhizomes; often occurs in clumps. Top-killed by fire but resprouts readily.

Names: Birch family, *Betulaceae*. *Betula* is the Latin name for birches; *glandulosa* refers to glands on the leaves. Also called resin, shrub, scrub, swamp and dwarf birch. Bog and swamp refer to its preferred habitat; shrub, scrub and dwarf refer to its small size and irregular growth form.

Compare with: other birches and alders, birchleaf mountain-mahogany, Pacific serviceberry.

Form: Perennial evergreen shrub with spreading habit and large thorns; commonly 2–5 feet tall.

Leaves: Simple, alternate, persistent. Ovate to elliptical; about 1 inch long; three-veined with rounded base; margins entire; tips acute to obtuse. Light gray-green above; pale gray-green and glabrous or slightly pubescent below, especially along veins (may need hand lens to see).

Flowers/fruit: Small, white flowers borne in dense clusters 1–2 inches long. Fruits are three-lobed capsules; ¼–½ inch in diameter; rough texture; slightly sticky when young. Small, hard seeds are ejected from the capsule when ripe.

Twigs/bark: Stems rigid and covered in white bloom; numerous stout thorns typically bear several leaves. Bark smooth; older bark whitish with yellow-green, spiny branchlets.

Range/habitat: Native to rocky ridges and open pine forests from southern Oregon to Baja, California; 2,000–11,000 feet. Common in chaparral shrub communities.

Notes: Spiny nature makes it difficult to work around. Improves site quality because it fixes nitrogen. Prolific seed producer; reproduces by seed, branch layering and sprouting from underground burls; fire stimulates seed germination. Pollinated by insects; birds, ants and rodents are important seed dispersers. Despite thorns, has browse value for deer, cattle, and domestic and wild sheep.

Names: Buckthorn family, *Rhamnaceae*. *Ceanothus* is Greek for a spiny plant; *cordulatus* refers to small, heart-shaped leaves. Also called mountain whitethorn and snow bush.

Compare with: other ceanothuses and manzanitas.

Form: Usually an erect evergreen shrub; 3–12 feet tall but can be prostrate, especially at higher elevations.

Leaves: Simple, opposite (but often in clusters), persistent. Small (¼–1 inch long); narrow; oblong to obovate; margins entire or with one to two teeth near apex; underside conspicuously veined; petiole very short. Gray-green to blue-green; generally smooth but often slightly pubescent below.

Flowers/fruit: Small, white to creamy white flowers borne in small, loose clusters (umbels). Fruits are rounded, three-lobed capsules; ¼ inch in diameter; each lobe has a horn near the apex; occur in clusters. Seeds are ejected up to 30 feet from the capsule, making an audible "pop"; receptacles remain attached to the twig.

Twigs/bark: Lateral branchlets opposite; short; stiff; often thornlike (but not true thorns); grow at right angles to main stem. Young twigs pubescent and red-brown; gray with age. Branches rigid and somewhat thorny. Bark gray and smooth; gray-brown with age.

Range/habitat: Grows from central Oregon southward through most of California, primarily on the west side of the Cascades and Sierras. Occurs on dry, rocky sites in full sun. Major component of chaparral brush fields, especially in California.

Notes: Does not sprout after fire (unlike most *Ceanothus* species), but fire stimulates seed germination; seeds can remain dormant in the soil for many years. Foliage is highly flammable; reproduction depends on fire. Important winter browse for deer, sheep and goats.

Names: Buckthorn family, *Rhamnaceae*. *Ceanothus* is Greek for a spiny plant; *cuneatus* means wedge-shaped. Also called greasewood, buckbrush, common buckbrush and wedgeleaf ceanothus.

Compare with: other ceanothuses and manzanitas.

Form: Erect, loosely branched deciduous shrub; typically 4–12 feet tall.

Leaves: Simple, alternate, deciduous (sometimes semipersistent). Small (1–3 inches long); oblong to ovate; margins generally entire but may be toothed; may have one or three prominent veins from base; petiole about ½ inch. Green to dark green and smooth above; paler green and smooth or sparsely pubescent below.

Flowers/fruit: Small, white to blue (rarely pink) flowers borne in long, terminal clusters (panicles). Fruits are rounded, three-lobed capsules; ¼ inch in diameter; each lobe has a ridge down its side; occur in clusters. Sticky seeds are ejected from the capsule when ripe.

Twigs/bark: Branches round; slender; frequently arching; green to tan. Bark gray-brown; warty on older branches.

Range/habitat: Occurs from 2,000–7,000 feet depending on latitude. Grows on many soil types but does best on well-drained, moderately fertile soil. Prefers open to partial sun; also found on dry slopes and ridges.

Notes: One of the most important browse species in the West; leaves are a good source of protein. Helps sites recover from fire because it fixes nitrogen; often used in streamside restoration. Reproduces by seed, sprouting and layering; seeds may remain viable in the soil for many years. Its supple branches are used to make baskets. May hybridize with other *Ceanothus* species.

Names: Buckthorn family, *Rhamnaceae*. *Ceanothus* is Greek for a spiny plant; *integerrimus* refers to smooth leaf margins. Also called deerbrush ceanothus.

Compare with: other ceanothuses and dogwoods.

Form: Prostrate evergreen shrub; forms dense, carpet-like mats to 10 feet wide. Branches often root at nodes.

Leaves: Simple, opposite, persistent. Small (¼–1-inch long); oblanceolate to obovate; narrow with sparse, sharp teeth (3–9) near apex; petiole very short; stipules persistent. Thick and leathery; dark green and shiny above; paler below with distinctive white bloom between secondary veins (appears as white dots).

Flowers/fruit: Small, blue to purple flowers borne in loose, terminal clusters (racemes). Fruits are almost-round capsules; ¼ inch in diameter; each lobe has a dorsal horn; occur in clusters.

Twigs/bark: Lateral branchlets short; rigid; spurlike; opposite; red-brown and hairy when young; gray and smooth with age. Bark red-brown and smooth; gray-brown with age.

Range/habitat: Grows in the Cascades of Washington, Oregon and northern California east into the mountains of Idaho and Nevada. Prefers dry sites in full sun, often in open mixed-conifer and ponderosa pine forests.

Notes: Provides some protection against erosion and acts as a nurse crop for seedlings. Low forage value.

Names: Buckthorn family, *Rhamnaceae. Ceanothus* is Greek for a spiny plant; *prostratus* refers to its prostrate growth form. Commonly known as squawcarpet, but this name is offensive to many and will be used less over time; also called prostrate ceanothus.

Compare with: other ceanothuses and manzanitas.

Form: Erect, loosely branched shrub with slender, red branches; 3–10 feet tall.

Leaves: Simple, alternate, deciduous. Ovate; 1–4 inches long; thin; margins serrated with glandular teeth; three-veined from base. Dark green and glabrous above; paler below.

Flowers/fruit: Small, white flowers borne in large, dense clusters to 5 inches long. Fruits are rounded, 3-lobed capsules; ³⁄₁₆ inch in diameter; occur in clusters. Seeds are ejected from the capsule when ripe.

Twigs/bark: Twigs slender; smooth; red to purple. Buds often stalked. Bark gray-brown.

Range/habitat: Grows from southern British Columbia to northern California and eastward into Montana on dry to moist, well-drained sites in sun or partial shade. Prefers more moisture than most *Ceanothus* species.

Notes: Important source of food and cover for many large and small mammals, including deer, elk, cattle and sheep. Birds, rodents and insects consume much of the annual seed crop. Seeds may remain dormant but viable in the soil for decades. Fire stimulates sprouting from the root collar and seed germination. Fixes nitrogen, which helps sites recover from fire.

Names: Buckthorn family, *Rhamnaceae*. *Ceanothus* is Greek for a spiny plant; *sanguineus* refers to its bloodred stems. Also called buckbrush because deer like to eat it and soapbloom because its flowers produce a soapy lather when beaten in water.

Compare with: other ceanothuses and dogwoods.

Form: Erect, stiffly branched shrub to 12 feet tall or small tree to 20 feet tall. May be low growing or prostrate on exposed sites.

Leaves: Simple, alternate (but small leaves are often grouped at the base of older leaves), persistent. Ovate to elliptical; ¾–2 inches long; margins finely serrated, gland-tipped, and sometimes revolute; prominently three-veined from base; petiole less than ½ inch. Dark glossy green above; paler below.

Flowers/fruit: Small, blue or lavender (rarely white) flowers borne in dense clusters to 3 inches long. Fruits are rounded, 3-lobed capsules; ³⁄₁₆ inch in diameter; sticky; almost black; occur in clusters. Capsule splits open to release tiny, smooth, black seeds.

Twigs/bark: Twigs slender; green; distinctly ribbed for two to three years then smooth and red-brown. Bark thin; red-brown; smooth roughening with age.

Range/habitat: Grows in coastal brush fields and forests from southwest Oregon through southern California on dry, well-drained sites in sun or shade.

Notes: Used ornamentally; its flowers contribute beauty to the forest. Leaves and young twigs are important browse for mule deer. Forms dense thickets after fire; pioneer species on disturbed sites. Fixes nitrogen and is drought tolerant.

Names: Buckthorn family, *Rhamnaceae*. *Ceanothus* is Greek for a spiny plant; *thyrsiflorus* refers to the arrangement of flowers, which resembles a thyrsus, the staff of Bacchus. Also called blueblossom, California-lilac, blue-brush and blue-myrtle.

Compare with: other ceanothuses and manzanitas.

Form: Erect or sprawling evergreen shrub with stout, green branches; to 10 feet tall. Often forms dense, impenetrable thickets, especially after forest fires.

Leaves: Simple, alternate, persistent. Ovate to ovate-elliptical; 1–3 inches long; margins serrated; 3-veined from base. Thick, dark green, and shiny above; paler green below. Sticky leaves emit a sickeningly sweet odor when rubbed or crushed, or in warm weather.

Flowers/fruit: Small, white flowers borne in large, dense clusters to 5 inches long. Fruits are rounded, 3-lobed capsules; ¼ inch in diameter; occur in clusters. Tiny, dark seeds have very hard seed coats; need high heat to germinate; ejected from the capsule when ripe.

Twigs/bark: Twigs stout; smooth; green. Older bark gray-brown; smooth.

Range/habitat: Widely distributed from southwest Canada through most western states. Occurs on a variety of sites and exposures from sea level to high mountains.

Notes: Invades burned and cutover land. Sprouts vigorously from root crown after damage; also reproduces by layering and seed; seeds can remain in the soil for decades (even 200 years) until fire stimulates seed germination. Fixes nitrogen; important nitrogen source for conifers and other trees but can also outcompete small trees. Its seeds are important food for birds and small mammals; animal seed caches play an important role in seed distribution. Indigenous people make hair and bath wash from the foamy flowers.

Names: Buckthorn family, *Rhamnaceae*. *Ceanothus* is Greek for a spiny plant; *velutinus* means velvety. Snowbrush refers to its clusters of white flowers. Also called snowbrush ceanothus, tobacco bush because it was smoked, and varnish-leaf ceanothus because of its shiny leaves.

Compare with: other ceanothuses and manzanitas.

Form: Erect shrub or small tree with distinctly crooked branches; to 30 feet tall.

Leaves: Simple, alternate, deciduous; two-ranked. Ovate to ovate-lanceolate; 1–4 inches long; margins serrated; base asymmetrical; apex acute to acuminate and often sickle-shaped; three main veins but netted between. Dark green above with stiff, sandpaper-like hairs; paler and pubescent along veins below.

Flowers/fruit: Tiny, green flowers borne singly on stalks in leaf axils. Fruits are small (about ¼ inch), round, dark brown to orange-red drupes; edible but not palatable.

Twigs/bark: Twigs round; crooked to zigzagged. Pith chambered at nodes. Terminal bud absent; lateral buds have imbricate scales. Bark red-brown to gray; ridged and furrowed; often warty.

Range/habitat: Grows east of the Cascade crest in Washington and Oregon, eastward into Oklahoma and Texas; most common in the Southwest. Grows on dry, gravelly soils, often on canyon slopes or near streams.

Notes: Its fruits are an important food source for birds and mammals; deer, antelope and beavers eat the leaves and branches. In southern part of range, dense thickets provide good hiding cover. Mistletoe often deforms branches into crooked masses. Some consider it a hybrid with southern and eastern hackberries. Used locally for firewood and fence posts; wood is hard to work, but early settlers fashioned it into furniture. Used ornamentally and in streamside restoration. Often sprouts abundantly after fire.

Names: Elm family, *Ulmaceae*. *Celtis* is from a Greek word for a tree bearing sweet fruit; *reticulata* means netted and refers to its leaf veins. Also called western hackberry and palo blanco.

Compare with: elms, but only in eastern part of range.

Form: Erect to spreading shrub to 20 feet tall; occasionally a small tree to 40 feet tall.

Leaves: Simple, alternate (commonly clustered on spur shoots), usually persistent (occasionally deciduous). Small (½–2 inches long); widely elliptical to obovate; conspicuously penniveined; margins typically serrated toward apex but entire toward base; petiole short (¼ inch). Vary from thin to thick; dark green to yellow-green and smooth above; paler and sometimes slightly pubescent below.

Flowers/fruit: Small, inconspicuous flowers borne in clusters of up to 12; perfect but lack petals; green calyx with yellow stamens. Fruits are slender achenes with long (to 3 inches), twisted, featherlike tails.

Twigs/bark: Twigs slender; red-brown and glaucous; gray with age; numerous spur shoots on older twigs. Mature bark thin; smooth; gray-brown.

Range/habitat: Grows on dry, sunny foothills and low mountain slopes from southwest Oregon into Mexico and eastward into Arizona. Common in chaparral communities and open pine and oak woodlands below 7,500 feet.

Notes: Used locally for fuel and turnery items. Good browse for deer and livestock. Indigenous people make red dye from the bark and use its hard wood for spears, arrows, clubs and digging tools. Extensive root systems probably fix nitrogen. Reproduces vegetatively from root crowns and rhizomes; seeds are not stored in the soil; successful germination depends on adequate moisture.

Names: Rose family, *Rosaceae*. *Cercocarpus* is derived from Greek and refers to seeds' plumed tails; *betuloides* refers to its birch-like leaves. Mountain-mahogany refers to its hard, red-brown wood. Also called birchleaf cercocarpus and true mountain-mahogany, although it is not related to true mahoganies. *C. montanus* is a synonym.

Compare with: curlleaf mountain-mahogany, bog birch.

Form: Erect, multibranched evergreen shrub or small tree to 35 feet tall.

Leaves: Simple, alternate (commonly clustered on spur shoots), persistent. Small (½–2 inches long); narrowly elliptical; margins entire and slightly revolute but often cupped up around the midrib; petiole very short. Thick and leathery; pubescent at first but smoother with age.

Flowers/fruit: Small, inconspicuous flowers borne in small clusters; perfect but lack petals; trumpet-shaped; pubescent; reddish calyx and stamens. Fruits are slender achenes with long (1–3 inches), twisted, featherlike tails.

Twigs/bark: Twigs slender; red-brown and glaucous; gray with age; numerous spur shoots on older twigs. Mature bark thick; furrowed; gray-brown.

Range/habitat: The most widely distributed mountain-mahogany. Inhabits dry coniferous forests and rangelands with large temperature fluctuations throughout western North America; 2,000–10,000 feet depending on latitude. Grows on rocky sites low in nutrients.

Notes: Shallow, spreading root system; root nodules contain nitrogen-fixing bacteria. Reproduces primarily by seed dispersed by wind and small animals; sprouting is not common. Pollinated primarily by wind. Long lived (sometimes more than 1,000 years). Important forage for big game. Its very hard wood sinks in water, burns hot and long, and was used to smelt ore. Indigenous people use decoctions of its bark and leaves to treat wounds and a variety of respiratory and internal diseases.

Names: Rose family, *Rosaceae*. *Cercocarpus* is derived from Greek and refers to seeds' plumed tails; *ledifolius* refers to leaves that resemble *Ledum* (wild rosemary). Mountain-mahogany refers to its hard, red-brown wood; curlleaf refers to revolute leaf margins. Also called curlleaf cercocarpus and desert mountain-mahogany. Not related to true mahoganies.

Compare with: birchleaf mountain-mahogany, bush chinquapin.

Form: Grows as a low, spreading, mounded evergreen shrub; 2-6 feet tall, but typically shorter. Can form dense thickets, especially in the montane chaparral in concert with other shrubs.

Leaves: Simple, alternate, and persistent (evergreen). Oblong to elliptical in shape, typically 1-3 inches long; margins are entire (not lobed or serrated). Top surface is dull gray-green; underside is rusty gold.

Flowers/fruit: Plant is monoecious and wind-pollinated; male flowers occur in elongated, creamy white catkins; female flowers are inconspicuous; flowers often foul smelling. Fruits are small clusters of spiny burrs 1–2 inches in diameter; each fruit contains one to three chestnut-like seeds. Seeds are eaten by birds, rodents and humans (raw or roasted). Seeds are dispersed by birds and mammals, both directly and when burs get stuck in their fur.

Twigs/bark: Typically thin, smooth, and gray or brown.

Range/habitat: Ranges from the mountains of southern Oregon into the Coast Ranges of northern California and throughout the Sierra Nevada mountains. Elevation ranges from 2,500 to 11,000 feet. Bush chinquapin is typically a midseral shrub occurring beneath dry conifer forests or in the montane chaparral; it prefers dry gravelly or rocky slopes. It survives fire by resprouting and can form fire-related (edaphic) climax communities where fire is frequent. If fire is excluded for long periods, it can eventually be shaded out by overtopping conifers.

Notes: An important food source for Native Americans, as well as many species of wildlife. Reproduces via seeds, but also spreads via rhizomes (underground stems).

Names: Beech family, Fagales. *Chrysolepis* (gold leaf) refers to the golden color of the undersides of its leaves, while *sempervirens* (always green or living) refers to its evergreen nature. Also called Sierra chinquapin. Chinquapin and chinkapin are alternative, and acceptable, common names; chinquapin is increasingly used because it is the older spelling. This genus was formerly called Castanopsis because of its similarity to the chestnut genus, *Castanea*.

Compare with: tanoak and golden chinquapin (especially in its shrubby form, *Chrysolepis chrysophylla* var. *minor*).

Form: Tough, fast-growing, woody vine to 50 feet tall. Often covers other plants, fences, sheds and abandoned cars.

Leaves: Pinnately compound, opposite, deciduous. Five to seven leaflets; oval to heart-shaped; margins lobed or unlobed and entire or toothed.

Flowers/fruit: White, fluffy flowers occur in masses for much of the summer; each flower has four to five white sepals but no petals; usually dioecious. Seeds have long, feathery tails; also occur in fluffy clusters.

Twigs/bark: Young twigs green and ribbed; tan with age. Older bark fibrous and stringy.

Range/habitat: Widely distributed west of the Mississippi River and in western Canada. In the Pacific Northwest, most common east of the Cascades in ponderosa pine forests and along roads and streams. Also occurs on the west side.

Notes: Its tough, stringy bark is woven into rope, mats and clothing. Indigenous people use its seed puffs in infant diapers, use infusions and washes to treat a variety of skin ailments, and chew the leaves to treat colds and sore throats. Some members of this genus have toxic properties, so use caution.

Names: Buttercup family, *Ranunculaceae. Clematis* comes from an ancient Greek word for a climbing vine; *ligusticifolia* refers to an Italian plant, *Ligusticum*, with similar foliage. Also called western white clematis, traveler's joy, old man's beard, virgin's bower, and pepper vine because early settlers sometimes used it as a substitute for pepper.

Compare with: orange honeysuckle, blue clematis.

Form: Large, spreading, loosely branched shrub; 3–20 feet tall. Forms dense thickets of intertwined plants.

Leaves: Simple, opposite, deciduous. Ovate; 2–6 inches long; margins entire to wavy; veins distinctively arcuate. Upper surface wrinkled; green above; paler green below; brilliant red in autumn. Leaves occur along entire stem, not in whorls near ends of branches as on many dogwoods.

Flowers/fruit: Small, white flowers borne in flat-topped clusters; each flower bears its own petals; not surrounded by large, white bracts like those in Pacific dogwood. Fruits are small (¼-inch), round, white to gray, single-seeded drupes.

Twigs/bark: Twigs slender; red to purple in sun but often green in shade; often red above and green below. Buds naked. Bark thin; red; prominent lenticels.

Range/habitat: One of the most widely distributed shrubs in North America. Grows on moist to wet sites along streams and rivers throughout much of North America at all but the highest elevations.

Notes: Many birds and mammals (especially moose) eat the leaves, twigs and fruits. Common ornamental because of its red twigs. The flexible stems are woven into baskets, fish traps, drying racks and the like. Leaves are sometimes smoked as tobacco and brewed as tea. Plants damaged by light fire or cutting sprout from base; light fire that removes duff may stimulate germination of buried seeds.

Names: Dogwood family, *Cornaceae*. *Cornus* is the Latin word for this genus; *sericea* means silky. The West Coast variety is commonly called western dogwood or creek dogwood and sometimes given the varietal name *occidentalis*, which means western. Formerly called *C. stolonifera*.

Compare with: other opposite-leaved plants such as dogwoods, honeysuckles and viburnums.

Form: Large, spreading deciduous shrub to 30 feet tall; stems to 12 inches in diameter.

Leaves: Simple, alternate, deciduous; two-ranked. Broadly ovate, obovate, or almost round; 2–4 inches long (larger in shade); margins sharply and doubly serrated. Dark green above; paler green below. Leaves, petioles, and young twigs are very fuzzy.

Flowers/fruit: Male and female flowers borne in separate catkins (aments) on the same plant; staminate catkins flower before leaves appear in spring; female catkins are very small with red stigmas. Fruits are nuts enclosed in a hairy, beaked husk that is much longer than the nut; commonly occur in clusters of two to four.

Twigs/bark: Branches zigzag between leaf nodes. Current-year twigs slender; brown; very pubescent. Bark thin; gray; smooth.

Range/habitat: One variety of *C. cornuta* just touches the eastern fringes of the Pacific Northwest; the California variety is widespread west of the Cascades and Sierras. Grows in the understory of coniferous forests, often on burned-over and cutover land. Common along streams and on other moist sites. Tolerant of shade and understory conditions.

Notes: Nuts are edible and can be mashed into cakes. Poor to fair browse value, but the nuts are a favorite of large birds and small mammals. Sprouts after low-severity fire, forming straight stems useful for basket weaving and arrow shafts. Related to commercial filbert but is a different species. Lewis and Clark were presented with hazelnuts when they arrived near The Dalles, Oregon. Compared with *C. cornuta*, variety *californica* has rounder leaves, glandular hairs on twigs and petioles, and a slightly shorter husk around the nut.

Names: Birch family, *Betulaceae*. *Corylus* is a Greek word for hazelnuts; *cornuta* means bearing horns and refers to the fruit husks. Our primary variety inhabits the West Coast, hence the varietal name *californica*.

Compare with: Common filbert (*C. avellana*) is a similar species, not native but often naturalized.

Form: Thicket-forming, thorny deciduous shrub to 10 feet tall or small tree to 35 feet tall; stems to 6 inches in diameter.

Leaves: Simple, alternate (commonly clustered on spur shoots), deciduous. Primarily ovate or obovate but sometimes elliptical; 1½–4 inches long; margins doubly serrated or lobed and serrated above midpoint but finely serrated or entire below midpoint; petiole grooved above, commonly with a leafy flange along sides. Green or yellow-green above; paler green below.

Flowers/fruit: Small, white flowers borne in large, showy clusters. Fruits are small (¼- to ½-inch) pomes; red, purple or black.

Twigs/bark: Twigs have sharp thorns that are soft when young but harden with age. Twigs red-brown and smooth; gray-brown with age. Terminal buds absent; lateral buds have bright red imbricate scales. Bark thin; red-brown; shallowly fissured; often scaly near base.

Range/habitat: Prefers moist, well-drained sites, often with sandy or gravelly soils.

Notes: Hybridizes with other hawthorns, making identification difficult. Sprouts and suckers from trunk and roots. Grows in dense thickets, providing cover for birds and small mammals; preferred nesting site for magpies. Variable browse value; wildlife eat its fruits. Indigenous people eat its fruits fresh and dried; use the fruits to treat heart, blood and circulation ailments; and use the thorns to lance blisters and boils, catch fish and pierce ears. According to legend, Paul Bunyon used it as a back scratcher.

Names: Rose family, *Rosaceae*. *Crataegus* means strength in Greek; *douglasii* honors Scottish botanist and plant explorer David Douglas. Also called Douglas or river hawthorn. Columbia hawthorn, *C. columbiana*, is now included within this species.

Compare with: oceanspray, other hawthorns.

Form: Erect, spreading, thorny deciduous shrub or small tree; 15–40 feet tall.

Leaves: Simple, alternate (often clustered on spur shoots), deciduous. Small (1–2 inches long); ovate; deeply lobed (almost to midrib) and serrated. Dark green above; paler green below.

Flowers/fruit: Small (¼- to ½-inch), white flowers borne in large, showy clusters of five to 25. Fruits are small (¼– to ½-inch), dark red pomes containing a single seed; edible; often called haws.

Twigs/bark: Twigs have sharp thorns that are soft when young but harden with age. Twigs red-brown and smooth; gray-brown with age. Terminal buds absent. Bark thin; gray-brown; shallowly fissured; often scaly near base.

Range/habitat: Native to Europe, Asia and Africa; now naturalized throughout much of the world, including most of North America. Highly invasive in fields and forests.

Notes: Fruits (called haws) are winter food for birds, which play an important role in distributing seeds (often along fencerows). Common ornamental; often used for hedgerows because of its dense branching and sharp thorns. Its fruits are often used in jam, jelly and syrup rather than eaten raw. In China, haws coated with spun sugar are treats. Hawthorns are powerful in myth, where they are used to slay vampires and mark the entrance to the other world. Many medicinal uses.

Names: Rose family, *Rosaceae*. *Crataegus* means strength in Greek; *monogyna* refers to one seed, as does the common name. This is the only hawthorn that contains a single seed. Also called English hawthorn and common hawthorn.

Compare with: oceanspray, other hawthorns.

Form: Erect deciduous shrub with slender, green branches; typically 3–12 feet tall. Often forms dense stands.

Leaves: Simple and trifoliate (on the same branch), alternate (single or in clusters), deciduous. Very small simple leaves (¼–½ inch long) or larger trifoliate leaves (to 1 inch long); elliptical to oblong; margins entire; sessile or petiolate. Light green and smooth above; paler green and slightly pubescent below.

Flowers/fruit: Small (about ¾ inch), bright yellow, pealike flowers; profuse; tripped open by pollinating bees and insects. Fruits are dark brown to black legumes; 1–3 inches long; pods twist open violently and noisily, expelling seeds. Small seeds have hard seed coats.

Twigs/bark: Twigs slender; green to dark green; distinctly ribbed; hairy when young; smooth with age. Green twigs photosynthesize; this is especially important when drought causes leaves to shed in hot weather. Bark gray-green; smooth; sometimes striped.

Range/habitat: Native to North Africa and Europe. Introduced to the United States in the 1800s, first as fodder for sheep and later as erosion control; now well established along both North American coasts. Highly invasive and difficult to control.

Notes: Commonly regarded as a noxious weed. May be toxic to wildlife and humans. Its root nodules fix nitrogen. Easily colonizes eroded and burned-over land as well as sandy soils along the coast. Ants gather its seeds and carry them to their nests; the seeds can be stored in the soil for many years. Its seedpod was the personal emblem of Charles VI of France.

Names: Legume family, *Fabaceae*. *Cytisus* comes from the Greek word for clover; *scoparius* is from the Anglo-Saxon word for broom. Also called English broom and written as one word, Scotchbroom.

Compare with: gorse and other introduced brooms.

Form: Short, sprawling deciduous shrub; erect to prostrate; typically less than 3 feet tall. Often grows in dense clumps on wet sites.

Leaves: Pinnately compound (three to seven leaflets), alternate, deciduous; often appear palmately compound until inspected closely. Leaflets typically less than 1 inch long; margins rolled under. Gray-green and velvety.

Flowers/fruit: Bright yellow, five-petaled flowers borne terminally; single or small clusters; about 1 inch in diameter; flowers most of the summer. Fruits are hairy achenes; occur in dense clusters; persist well into winter.

Twigs/bark: First-year twigs covered in silky hairs. Bark red-brown; fibrous.

Range/habitat: Widely distributed across the Northern Hemisphere. Occupies a wide variety of site conditions; in the Pacific Northwest, occurs primarily in wet meadows along the edges of coniferous forests east of the Cascades. Grows as a stunted "cushion plant" at high elevations.

Notes: Low forage value but commonly browsed; birds and small mammals eat its seeds. Often used in restoration projects on disturbed sites, such as mining operations and roadsides. Common ornamental where cold hardiness is important. Reproduces by windblown seeds and sprouts from root crown and prostrate stems. Early to late-successional species. Susceptible to fire but resprouts easily if not killed. Indigenous people use it, often as a tea, to treat many ailments; the fibrous bark can be used to start fires.

Names: Rose family, *Rosaceae*. *Dasiphora* is a genus of three shrubs native to Asia and beyond; *fruticosa* means shrubby. Cinquefoil refers to five leaflets. Also called bush cinquefoil. *Potentilla* is a synonym for *Dasiphora*.

Compare with: buttercups (herbaceous), Scotch broom.

Form: Erect deciduous shrub with multiple slender stems; often grows in rounded mounds several feet tall but may reach 12 feet.

Leaves: Simple, alternate, deciduous. Long and narrow (to 2½ inches long, ⅛ inch wide); margins entire; grasslike; sessile. Gray-green and pubescent (often densely) on both surfaces; not distinctly aromatic.

Flowers/fruit: Small, yellow, conical flowers borne in rounded clusters. Fruits are small, single-tufted achenes with angled or ribbed sides. Flowers and fruits in August through October, often simultaneously.

Twigs/bark: Young twigs slender; round; gray to light yellow; pubescent. Cut twigs exude a milky latex that contains a high-grade rubber called chrysil.

Range/habitat: Ranges from southern Canada into Mexico and from the Great Plains to the Pacific Ocean; common in plains, foothills and valleys of the dry Intermountain West; 0–10,000 feet. Common in open range and open ponderosa pine and juniper forests.

Notes: Forage value varies dramatically depending on season and animal; summer use often low; winter use higher. Provides important cover for ground-nesting birds. Reproduces by seed and sprouting. Early successional species; rapidly colonizes disturbed sites; commonly enhanced by fire. Excellent for soil stabilization and erosion control. Tolerant of extreme cold, moisture stress and high salt content in soil. Once experimented with for potential value in rubber production but found unsuitable.

Names: Aster family, *Asteraceae*. *Ericameria* is from the Greek words *ereike* and *meris* and refers to heathlike leaves; *nauseosa* refers to the disagreeable taste of its leaves and stems. Also called gray or grey rabbitbrush, goldenbush and chamisa. Also called *Chrysothamnus nauseosus*. Many subspecies, races and ecotypes with highly variable characteristics and names.

Compare with: big sagebrush, bitterbrush, other rabbitbrushes.

Form: Erect, highly branched evergreen shrub to 10 feet tall. Sometimes a small tree to 20 feet tall.

Leaves: Simple, opposite, persistent. Elliptical; 2–4 inches long; margins entire but wavy and revolute; petiole short and stiff. Thick and leathery; dark green above; paler green with wooly, silver pubescence below.

Flowers/fruit: Flowers borne in unisexual cascading catkins (aments) on separate plants. Catkins form in fall and contrast with foliage throughout winter; male catkins long (to 12 inches), yellowish when young, and gray with age; female catkins shorter (2–4 inches) and silver-gray. Fruits are small (about ¼ inch), round, blue to black berries; dry and brittle when mature; each contains two seeds borne by cottony puffs.

Twigs/bark: Opposite branching. Twigs slender to moderately stout; green or red when young; olive green then red-brown-gray with age. Bark thin; gray; smooth except for lenticels.

Range/habitat: Grows on bluffs, dunes, chaparral and pine-oak woodlands in coastal Oregon and California; 0–2,500 feet.

Notes: Not commonly browsed. Popular ornamental because of its evergreen nature, dramatic cascading flowers and striking purple fruits. Indigenous people use its fire-hardened wood to pry mussels off rocks along the coast.

Names: Silk-Tassel family, *Garryaceae*. *Garrya* commemorates Nicholas Gary, secretary of the Hudson's Bay Company; *elliptica* refers to elliptical leaves. Wavyleaf refers to its wavy leaf margins, which help distinguish it from Fremont silktassel. Also called coast silktassel.

Compare with: Fremont's silktassel, salal.

Form: Erect, highly branched evergreen shrub to 10 feet tall; sometimes a small tree. Typically occurs as scattered individuals.

Leaves: Simple, opposite, persistent. Oval, ovate, or obovate; 1–4 inches long; ½–2 inches wide; margins entire and not wavy; petiole about ½ inch. Thick and leathery; light yellow-green and glabrous above; paler green and pubescent or glabrous below.

Flowers/fruit: Small, paired flowers borne in long, pendent spikes (catkins/aments); covered in dense, purple-gray pubescence; lack petals; male and female catkins borne on separate plants (dioecious). Fruits are small (about ¼ inch), round, blue to black berries; each usually bears two seeds; glabrous to slightly pubescent.

Twigs/bark: Opposite branching. Twigs slender to moderately stout; light yellow-green to red-green in sun; glabrous. Older branches and stems drab olive-gray.

Range/habitat: Found on dry, sunny sites in western Oregon and California; more common in southwest Oregon and California high chaparral communities; 2,500–7,000 feet.

Notes: Important winter and spring browse for mule deer and some livestock; many birds and rodents eat its fruits. Often used ornamentally because of its showy flowers and fruit. Early settlers used an extract as a tonic. Reproduces by seed and basal sprouts. Recovers from fire by sprouting, but fire often kills seeds. Found through all stages of succession but seems favored by frequent fire.

Names: Silk-Tassel family, *Garryaceae*. *Garrya* commemorates Nicholas Gary, secretary of the Hudson's Bay Company; *fremontii* commemorates John C. Fremont, noted military leader, explorer of the American West, and one of the first senators from California. Also called bear brush, flannel bush and quinine bush.

Compare with: wavyleaf silktassel, salal.

Form: Evergreen shrub; height varies depending on light. Forms dense, low thickets 1–3 feet tall in full sun; spindly and reaches 10 feet tall in shade.

Leaves: Simple, alternate, persistent. Ovate to oval; 2–4 inches long; margins finely serrated; primary lateral veins sparse and arcuate; minor veins netted; petiole very short. Leathery; dark glossy green above; paler green below.

Flowers/fruit: Small (¼-inch), urn-shaped, pink to white flowers borne in elongated clusters. Fruits are small (¼ inch), round, blue-black berries; edible but variable in flavor.

Twigs/bark: Twigs zigzag between nodes. Young twigs green to red, covered in short hairs. Older twigs gray-brown, smooth. Bark seldom seen because of its thicket-forming nature; red-brown to gray-brown, longitudinally scaly.

Range/habitat: Perhaps the most common shrub west of the Cascade crest, almost regardless of light and moisture; also common throughout coastal California. Commonly dominates the understory because of its dense, underground mats of rhizomes.

Notes: Sprouts profusely from rhizomes, forming dense, impenetrable thickets. Its fruits are eaten by birds, small mammals and humans (especially in jam and jelly). The foliage is used in floral arrangements and an important export item to European flower markets. Forage for deer, elk and black bears; mountain beavers use its leaves for nests. Lewis and Clark were presented with salal syrup on their trip west.

Names: Heath family, *Ericaceae. Gaultheria* is named after French botanist Jean-Francois Gaultier; *shallon* is from a Chinook word for this plant, *kikwu-salu,* which is also the source of the common name, salal.

Compare with: silktassel, evergreen huckleberry.

Form: Erect, loosely branched shrub to 15 feet tall. Typically has multiple straight and arching stems arising from base.

Leaves: Simple, alternate, deciduous. Small (1–3 inches long); ovate; coarsely toothed or lobed and serrated; margins entire near base; prominently penniveined. Green above; paler below.

Flowers/fruit: Tiny, creamy white flowers borne in large, loose, hanging clusters to 12 inches long. Fruits are tiny, light brown, one-seeded follicles; occur in large clusters; persist through winter and into the next growing season. Seeds are small and hairy.

Twigs/bark: Twigs slightly ridged when young, round with age. Pith large, white and spongy. Basal spouts very straight; used for arrow shafts. Bark smooth, gray-brown.

Range/habitat: Grows on well-drained, dry sites in sun and shade, often on shallow, rocky soils. Tolerant of shade and understory conditions.

Notes: Browsed by elk and deer. Sprouts from root crown and rhizomes after fire. Indigenous people use a mixture of its bark and leaves to treat burns. Before nails, oceanspray pegs were used in construction. The wood was sometimes used to make knitting needles.

Names: Rose family, *Rosaceae*. *Holodiscus* is from the Greek words *holos* and *diskos* meaning the entire disc; *discolor* means of varying colors and probably refers to tops and bottoms of the leaves. Oceanspray refers to its flower color; the large flower clusters remind some of the spray from ocean waves. Also called arrow-wood because of its use in arrow and spear shafts, ironwood because of its wood strength and creambush because of its flower color.

Compare with: hawthorns.

Form: Trailing, mat-forming coniferous shrub; seldom more than 3 feet tall; grows in densely matted clumps that may reach 10–12 feet in diameter. Sometimes a small tree, especially in Scandinavia.

Leaves: Short (¼- to ½-inch long), evergreen needles; needlelike to lancelike; commonly curved; mostly in whorls of three around twig (six-ranked), but some are opposite and four-ranked. Stiff and prickly; white bloom on one side; green on the other.

Cones: Male and female cones usually, but not always, occur on separate plants (dioecious). Male cones shed yellow pollen then wither and die. Female cones are berrylike rather than woody and take two seasons to mature; first-year cones green; second-year cones blue-black; both covered in white bloom. Seeds are wingless.

Twigs/bark: Twigs stiff and green; red-brown with age. Bark thin, shreddy, red-brown to dark brown.

Range/habitat: Perhaps the most widely distributed woody plant in the world. The only conifer species native to North America, Europe and Asia. Common at high latitudes and high altitudes throughout the Northern Hemisphere but also grows along coastlines; ranges from lowland bogs to alpine tundra. Prefers dry, open sites such as rocky ridges and outcrops.

Notes: Indigenous people use decoctions of its foliage, twigs and berries to treat ailments ranging from tuberculosis to coughs and colds. The berries flavor food and drink, including modern gin. Low browse value, but birds and mammals eat its fruits and play a key role in seed distribution. Digestion may aid seed germination. The resinous foliage is susceptible to fire damage.

Names: Cypress family, *Cupressaceae*. *Juniperus* is the Latin name for this group of plants; *communis* refers to its common occurrence. Also called ground, prostrate and dwarf juniper.

Compare with: other junipers.

Form: Widely branched, climbing or sprawling vine to 20 feet long.

Leaves: Simple, opposite (terminal pair fused into a single disk), deciduous. Oval; 2–4 inches long; margins entire but have fine hairs. Green to blue-green above; whitish bloom below.

Flowers/fruit: Orange-yellow, narrow, trumpet-shaped flowers borne in whorls above terminal leaf disk; 1–2 inches long. Fruits are orange-red, translucent berries with several seeds. They occur in small bunches above terminal leaf disk. Reports of edibility vary from edible to mildly poisonous, so don't take chances.

Twigs/bark: Twigs thin; vinelike; commonly twist around one another; tan with red tinges; covered in white bloom when young; pith hollow. Bark not commonly seen; thin; red-brown; often shreddy.

Range/habitat: Widespread throughout coniferous forests of the Intermountain West but not particularly common. More common west of the Cascades than east. Found at mid to low elevations.

Notes: Its flowers lack fragrance and rely on color and nectar to attract pollinators (primarily hummingbirds). Birds and mammals eat its fruits; children often suck nectar from the flowers. Indigenous people have many uses for this plant, including treating epilepsy, tuberculosis and colds; healing bruises; washing hair; and making string and twine. Some put its vines under their pillows to induce sleep.

Names: Honeysuckle family, *Caprifoliaceae*. *Lonicera* commemorates German botanist Adam Lonitzer; *ciliosa* refers to hairs along leaf margins. Also called orange honeysuckle.

Compare with: other honeysuckles, white clematis.

Form: Erect deciduous shrub to 5 feet tall.

Leaves: Simple, opposite, deciduous. Elliptical to nearly round (1–3 inches long); margins entire; apex round to acute. Covered in fine hairs.

Flowers/fruit: Small (¼- to ½-inch), dark red to purple flowers borne on long, upright stalks; paired; strongly two-lipped with upper lip erect and lower lip reflexed. Fruits are bright red, translucent berries; ¼–½ inch in diameter. They occur in pairs with fruits commonly fused together. Each pair occurs on a long, upright stalk.

Twigs/bark: Branches square in cross-section. They are green when young, eventually turning tan, then gray-brown.

Range/habitat: Occurs in Washington, Oregon and California, becoming more common southward. Not common in Oregon and Washington except in local spots. (Feel lucky if you find some!) Generally found at mid to high elevations. Grows along streams, in subalpine forest openings and on open, rocky slopes and talus.

Notes: Eaten by some, but not all, Indigenous people.

Names: Honeysuckle family, *Caprifoliaceae*. *Lonicera* commemorates German botanist Adam Lonitzer; *conjugialis* is Latin for marriage and refers to its conjoined fruits. Also called double honeysuckle and mountain twinberry.

Compare with: other honeysuckles, buffaloberry, huckleberries.

Form: Climbing or sprawling vine to 20 feet long.

Leaves: Simple, opposite, deciduous; one or more pairs at the terminal end fused into disks. Oval; 1–3 inches long; margins entire with fine hairs. Green above; blue-white below; pubescent on both surfaces.

Flowers/fruit: Pink to purple, narrow, trumpet-shaped flowers borne in long-stemmed clusters above terminal leaf disk; 1–2 inches long; distinctly two-lipped. Fruits are red, translucent berries with several seeds; occur in small bunches above terminal leaf disk; reports of edibility vary from edible to mildly poisonous, so don't take chances.

Twigs/bark: Twigs thin; vinelike; commonly twist around one another; purple; covered in bloom and fine hairs when young; smooth with age; pith hollow. Bark not commonly seen; thin; gray-brown; often shreddy.

Range/habitat: Occurs from southern British Columbia to southern California, primarily west of the Cascades and Sierras; more common in the south; mid to low elevations (generally below 3,500 feet); often grows on drier sites in canyons, open woodlands and coniferous forests. Grows as a trailing vine in open forests and thickets; climbs trees.

Notes: Host for the pathogen that causes sudden oak death (*Phytophthora ramorum*). Likely to be top-killed by fire but will resprout from base unless fire is too hot. Berries are eaten by wildlife but bitter to humans and may be mildly toxic. Indigenous people use the hollow stems as pipe stems and burned ashes for tattooing. Its flowers attract hummingbirds, butterflies and bees.

Names: Honeysuckle family, *Caprifoliaceae*. *Lonicera* commemorates German botanist Adam Lonitzer; *hispidula* means finely bristled and refers to the numerous hairs on its leaves and stems. Also called California and hairy honeysuckle.

Compare with: other honeysuckles, white clematis.

Form: Erect to straggly deciduous shrub to 10 feet tall. Forms dense thickets along the coast.

Leaves: Simple, opposite, deciduous. Ovate to elliptical; 2–5 inches long; tips pointed; margins entire; veins arcuate. Green and smooth above; smooth or sometimes hairy below.

Flowers/fruit: Small (½-inch), yellow, tubular or trumpet-shaped flowers surrounded by two bracts that become red to purple; occur in pairs. Fruits are purple to black berries surrounded by maroon bracts, about ¼ inch in diameter. Fruits occur in pairs. They are not edible and sometimes listed as toxic.

Twigs/bark: Twigs opposite; four-angled; light yellow-green; red-brown with age. Bark yellow-gray to gray-brown; shreddy.

Range/habitat: The most common and widely distributed honeysuckle in the West. Grows across Canada and most western states; sea level to subalpine. Most common on moist sites near streams and lakes; often grows on wet sites with willows and alders. Grows in sun and shade but is most vigorous in sun.

Notes: Its flowers attract hummingbirds and butterflies. Birds and mammals eat the berries; humans do not. Some thought its berries caused craziness, but others used them to purge the body and treat a variety of ailments. Indigenous people use berries for black dyes, including hair color.

Names: Honeysuckle family, *Caprifoliaceae*. *Lonicera* commemorates German botanist Adam Lonitzer; *involucrata* refers to the involucre of bracts surrounding the flower. Also called bearberry, California honeysuckle, twinberry and four-line honeysuckle.

Compare with: other honeysuckles, Indian-plum, white-flowered rhododendron.

Form: Thicket-forming shrub or small tree to 40 feet tall.

Leaves: Simple, alternate (commonly clustered on spur shoots), deciduous. Small (1–4 inches); ovate to elliptical; lobed (typically three lobes) and unlobed leaves on same branch; margins serrated and often curve upward around the midrib; petiole stout, about 1 inch long. Green to yellow-green and smooth above; paler and somewhat pubescent below.

Flowers/fruit: Small (½-inch), fragrant, white to pink flowers borne in clusters. Fruits are round to egg-shaped pomes (apples); about ½ inch in diameter; yellow, brown, or purple-red; edible but typically sour.

Twigs/bark: Twigs moderately slender; pubescent the first season but smooth later; red-brown when young; gray-brown with age. Spur shoots abundant on older branches; sometimes resemble thorns. Bark gray-brown; shreddy.

Range/habitat: Ranges from southern Alaska to San Francisco, hugging the coast farther south; generally below 3,000 feet. Most common near streams, lakes and ponds. Sun or partial shade.

Notes: Sprouts from base and roots; resulting thickets provide excellent cover for wildlife. Browsed by deer, elk and bears. Birds and small mammals eat its fruits, but small fruit size minimizes human use. Indigenous people use tonics and decoctions for internal aliments and eyewash and eat the fruits raw or store them for winter. Its bark and seeds contain cyanide compounds. The tough, fine-grained wood is sometimes used for turnery items.

Names: Rose family, *Rosaceae. Malus* is the name Romans used for apple trees; *fusca* means dusky brown and probably refers to fruit color. Also called western and Pacific crabapple; Oregon, western and Pacific all refer to its native range. Crabapple may be written as one or two words.

Compare with: hawthorns, cherries, ninebark, oceanspray.

Form: Erect but often straggly, spreading deciduous shrub; 3–8 feet tall.

Leaves: Simple, alternate (often clustered along branches and at branch tips), deciduous. Elliptical to obovate; 1–3 inches long; margins wavy and finely toothed. The nipple-like tip of midrib protrudes beyond the blade. Apex and base are acute; petiole is ¼ inch and pubescent. Dark green to blue-green above and paler green below. Leaves are sparsely pubescent on both surfaces and scarlet red in fall. They emit a skunky smell when crushed.

Flowers/fruit: Small (¼- to ½-inch), urn-shaped flowers borne in drooping, terminal clusters on previous year's growth; yellow-white to salmon to pink corolla. Fruits are small (about ¼-inch long), oval, four-parted capsules.

Twigs/bark: Young twigs are slender, yellow-tan and covered in sticky, rust-colored hairs. Mature bark is gray-red-brown and shreddy.

Range/habitat: Grows on moist but well-drained sites in shady to open coniferous forests in most western states, from sea level to high elevations. Tolerates shade and cold, wet sites. May be common locally but is often an infrequent member of Pacific Northwest forests.

Notes: Poisonous to livestock if eaten in large quantities but browsed by deer, elk and moose. Its strikingly blue foliage is easy to notice in the woods. Reproduces by seed, sprouting and layering. It often has a difficult time recovering from logging activities. Indigenous people chew its leaves to lessen heart pain and ease indigestion. Forked twigs were used to foster love.

Names: Heath family, *Ericaceae. Menziesia* commemorates Archibald Menzies, Scottish surgeon and botanist. *Ferruginea* means rust-colored and refers to the rust-colored hairs on branches and leaves. Also called false azalea and fool's huckleberry because of its resemblance to these plants.

Compare with: rhododendrons; azaleas, black twinberry, Indian-plum, some huckleberries.

Form: Large evergreen shrub or small tree to 30 feet tall and 1foot in diameter.

Leaves: Simple, alternate, persistent. Narrowly elliptical (2–4 inches long, ½–¾-inch wide). Margins regularly toothed and revolute except near base; teeth may be pointed or rounded. Leathery; dark green and smooth above; paler green below. Bottom surface has minute, black or white dots; may be fragrant when crushed.

Flowers/fruit: Male and female flowers usually borne in unisexual catkins (aments) in leaf axils on the same plant; both catkins ½–1 inch long. Fruits are small (¹/₁₆-inch), round, waxy drupes, dark purple but often covered in white or gray wax. They usually occur in small, tight clusters.

Twigs/bark: Young twigs are dark green, pubescent and slightly ridged. Older twigs are round, brown to gray and moderately stout. Bark is thin, gray to brown, often covered in white patches.

Range/habitat: Grows on moist but well-drained soils in sun or shade near sea level from Vancouver Island through California. Very shade tolerant.

Notes: Early settlers gathered its fruits and rendered wax to make candles, but production was often low. Indigenous people use the bark and leaves to treat digestive ailments. Its root nodules fix nitrogen, allowing growth on sandy and poor soils. Common ornamental.

Names: Wax-Myrtle family, *Myricaceae*. *Myrica* refers to a Greek plant with greasy fruit; *californica* refers to its range along the West Coast of North America. Also called California bayberry; bayberry and waxmyrtle are often used interchangeably in the common name. The common names refer to its wax-covered fruits and fragrant leaves. Some classify it as *Morella* rather than *Myrica*.

Compare with: California-laurel, tanoak, willows.

Form: Erect, loosely branched deciduous shrub to 15 feet tall.

Leaves: Simple, alternate, deciduous. Generally elliptical or oblong (resemble rabbit ears); 2–5 inches long; margins entire to wavy. Light green and smooth above; paler green below; fresh foliage smells and tastes like cucumber or watermelon rind; older foliage is bitter. Among the first plants to leaf out in spring.

Flowers/fruit: Small, green-white, imperfect flowers hang in long clusters; male and female flowers borne on separate plants (dioecious). Fruits are small (to ½-inch long), ovoid drupes; orange or yellow when young; blue-black when mature; typically occur in clusters with multiple colors at the same time.

Twigs/bark: Twigs slender and green; red-brown with age; conspicuous, orange lenticels. Pith chambered. Bark smooth and red-brown to dark gray.

Range/habitat: Grows on moist, well-drained sites in sun or shade west of the Cascade crest. Especially common along streams and in open woods at low elevations.

Notes: Generally considered poor forage, but birds, foxes, coyotes and other mammals eat its fruits, often before they mature. Indigenous people eat its fruits fresh and dried; medicinal uses include purging the body and treating burns and tuberculosis. Reproduces by seed and suckering. Valuable in streamside restoration because it thrives in wet, shady spots.

Names: Rose family, *Rosaceae*. *Oemleria* means pathway; *ceraciformis* means cherry-shaped. Indian-plum refers to its small, plumlike fruit. Sometimes called oso berry, bird cherry or skunk bush.

Compare with: black twinberry or cherries.

Form: Erect or semiprostrate shrub with 1 or more upright stems; 3–12 feet tall.

Leaves: Simple, alternate, deciduous; typically clustered near ends of stems. Large (5–15 inches in diameter); palmately lobed (maple-like). Bright green above; paler green below. Leaves and leaf veins heavily armed with long, fine, irritating prickles.

Flowers/fruit: Small, white flowers borne in large, upright, conical, terminal clusters 3–6 inches long. Fruits are bright red, flattened, ellipsoidal drupes; occur in upright, terminal clusters; not edible.

Twigs/bark: Stems sparse; upright; thick (½ inch or more in diameter); tan; heavily armed with slender, stiff, irritating prickles. Bark tan; heavily armed.

Range/habitat: Widespread in the Pacific Northwest and western provinces of Canada. Disjunct populations occur in the northern Great Lakes region. Occurs on wet sites, such as streams, seeps or avalanche tracks, in full sun or dense shade. Typically indicates a late seral forest of western hemlock or western redcedar.

Notes: Bear, elk and deer eat its fruits, leaves and stems. Slugs climb over the spines to eat its leaves. Devilsclub is strong medicine for many Indigenous people, who use it to cure a wide array of ailments. Sticks and ashes are used to ward off evil spirits. Wood is used for fishing lures because it floats and is easy to work. Its large leaves help keep Pacific Northwest streams cool for fish.

Names: Ginseng family, *Araliaceae*. *Oplopanax* is from the Greek words *hoplon*, for weapon, and *panax*, for ginseng, to which it is related; *horridus* (also spelled *horridum*) refers to its prickly nature. Devilsclub refers to the heavily armed stems. Also written as devil's club. An eastern relative is called devil's walking stick. Sometimes *horridum* is used for the specific epithet.

Compare with: bigleaf maple, thimbleberry, stink currant.

Form: Short evergreen shrub; 1–3 feet tall; sparse to dense.

Leaves: Simple, opposite (or nearly so), persistent. Small (½–1½ inches long); ovate to elliptical (sometimes obovate or spatulate); margins finely toothed and often slightly rolled under; petiole short (¹⁄₁₆ inch). Thick and leathery; dark green, glossy and smooth above; paler green below.

Flowers/fruit: Very small, maroon, highly fragrant flowers borne in small, axillary clusters. (Feel lucky if you see them.) Fruits are white, oval, one- to two-seeded capsules; about ¼ inch long; covered by a white, fleshy aril.

Twigs/bark: Twigs opposite; thin but stiff; red-brown; four-ridged for one to two years; round with age; no pubescence. Branches spreading or ascending. Buds small; round. Mature bark gray; smooth; prominent lenticels.

Range/habitat: Inhabits dry to moist coniferous forests at mid to high elevations but also grows at sea level in California. Usually indicates cool, well-drained sites.

Notes: Important forage for deer, elk, moose and mountain sheep despite low nutritional value; not important for domestic animals. Common ornamental; sometimes used in floral arrangements. Reproduces by seed and branch layering. Sprouts from taproot and root crown after light fire but can be killed by hot fires.

Names: Bittersweet family, *Celastraceae*. Genus also spelled *Pachystima* and *Pachistima*; all forms are from the Greek words *pachy*, for thick, and *stima*, for stigma (part of the flower stalk); *myrsinites* refers to its resemblance to the genus *Myrsine*. Also called mountain lover, falsebox, mountain boxwood, boxleaf and boxleaf myrtle.

Compare with: kinnikinnick, pipsissewa, some huckleberries.

Form: Erect, loosely branched deciduous shrub to 12 feet tall.

Leaves: Simple, opposite, deciduous. Ovate; 1–3 inches long; margins nearly entire with several glandular teeth on each side; three (rarely five) conspicuous veins arise from base. Green above; paler green below; somewhat hairy margins and veins.

Flowers/fruit: Numerous showy, white flowers; solitary or clustered; about 1 inch in diameter; fragrant. Fruits are small (¼-inch long), brown, four-chambered capsules; often in clusters.

Twigs/bark: Twigs slender; opposite; tan; widely dichotomous. Bark generally light brown and smooth; may check and shed with age.

Range/habitat: Ranges from southern British Columbia through central California and east into western Montana; sea level to 7,000 feet. Prefers moist, well-drained sites in sun or open coniferous forests; also occurs on drier sites. Often, but not always, associated with moist draws and riparian areas.

Notes: Common ornamental because of its showy, fragrant flowers. Leaves and flowers foam into a lather when crushed and rubbed vigorously. Its straight stems are used for bows, arrows, pipe stems, shuttles for weaving and knitting needles. Low browse value, but deer and elk sometimes browse the leaves. Birds and small mammals eat its seeds. Reproduces by seed and vegetatively; seeds accumulate in a soil-based seed bank. Sprouts from root crown even when top is killed by fire. State flower of Idaho.

Names: Hydrangea family, *Hyrdrangeaceae*. *Philadelphus* refers to a Greek king of Egypt; *lewisii* commemorates Merriweather Lewis. Also called syringa and Lewis' mockorange. Mockorange should be written as one word or hyphenated to show it's not related to true oranges.

Compare with: dogwoods, viburnums, honeysuckles, western wahoo.

Form: Large, erect, spreading, broadleaved deciduous shrub; 3–12 feet tall.

Leaves: Simple, alternate, deciduous. Palmately lobed (maple-like); three or five pointed (sometimes rounded) lobes; 1½–5 inches in diameter; petioles ¾–1½ inches. Dark green above; paler green and somewhat pubescent below.

Flowers/fruit: Small (¼-inch), white flowers borne in dense, upright, hemispherical clusters. Fruits are small (¼-inch long), red-brown follicles, occurring in dense, upright hemispherical clusters. Fruits split open as seeds ripen.

Twigs/bark: Young twigs slender; orange-brown; tight bark. On older twigs, bark splits and exfoliates in many-layered long strips but remains thin and yellow- or orange-brown.

Range/habitat: Range extends into California, Montana and Utah. Occurs on moist, well-drained sites in sun or shade at mid and low elevations, often with thimbleberry and western dogwood. Common along streams but can tolerate drier conditions.

Notes: Inferior browse value for most species. Indigenous people use its bark in a tea to induce vomiting and purge the body. They use straight shoots to make bows and arrows for children. Common ornamental; spring flowers and fall leaf color can be spectacular.

Names: Rose family, *Rosaceae*. *Physocarpus* comes from the Greek words *physa*, for bladder, and *karpos*, for fruit; *capitatus* refers to its round-headed fruit. Ninebark refers to the numerous layers of bark on the stem. Also called Pacific ninebark. Similar to mallow ninebark, *Philadelphus malvaceus*, which is common east of the Cascades.

Compare with: maples, currants, thimbleberry, oceanspray and other ninebarks.

Form: Thicket-forming shrub or small tree to 40 feet tall.

Leaves: Simple, alternate, deciduous. Oblong to oval; 1–3 inches long; finely toothed; apex rounded; one to two small glands on leaf base.

Flowers/fruit: Small (½-inch), fragrant, white to pink flowers borne in flat-topped clusters of five to 10. Fruits are bright red cherries with a single seed; ¼–½ inch in diameter; typically bitter (edible but not tasty). Seeds contain cyanide and should not be swallowed in large numbers.

Twigs/bark: Young twigs moderately slender and red-brown; gray-brown with age. Short spur shoots on older branches. Bark red-brown; gray with age; shiny; prominent, horizontal lenticels.

Range/habitat: Occurs in a variety of moist forests and along streams at low to mid elevations from British Columbia through most of the West. Relatively shade intolerant.

Notes: Valuable browse for large mammals, including cattle and sheep; most animals eat its fruits. Indigenous people use horizontal strips of the tough, stringy bark to bind implements and as decoration in baskets. They also boil the inner bark to alleviate heart trouble and use its fruits as laxatives. Adapts well to disturbed and degraded sites; often used in restoration projects. Early successional species. Seeds are widely dispersed by birds and mammals and may remain viable in the soil for many years. Sprouts readily from root crown and roots; sprouts vigorously after fire.

Names: Rose family, *Rosaceae*. *Prunus* is the Latin name for the genus that includes cherries, plums, peaches, apricots and almonds, among others; *emarginata* refers to serrated leaf margins. Bitter refers to the taste of its fruits.

Compare with: other cherries and plums; apples and crabapples; buckthorns.

Form: Thicket-forming shrub or small tree to 25 feet tall.

Leaves: Simple, alternate, deciduous. Elliptical to broadly ovate; 1–2 inches long; margins finely serrated; apex rounded; base rounded to heart-shaped; one or more glands on petiole or base. Somewhat thickened; dark green, smooth and lustrous above; paler below.

Flowers/fruit: Small, white flowers borne in loose, round clusters of one to seven. Fruits are oblong drupes; yellow, dark red, or purple; ½–1½ inches long; ridged on one side; edible but tart.

Twigs/bark: Twigs slender; eventually red-brown; smooth; conspicuous lenticels. Older branches gray-brown; numerous spur shoots, some of which resemble thorns. Often described as stiff and spiny. Bark thin; gray-brown; fissured and broken into scaly plates.

Range/habitat: Occurs in coniferous and mixed-evergreen forests from western Oregon to central California on dry to moist but well-drained sites; 0–6,000 feet. Shade intolerant.

Notes: Sprouts from roots, often forming dense thickets. Associated with black hawthorn, Oregon crabapple, chokecherry and ponderosa pine. Fruits make excellent jam and jelly. Indigenous people eat its fruits fresh and dried and make green dye from the leaves. Good browse value. Insects pollinate the flowers.

Names: Rose family, *Rosaceae*. *Prunus* is the Latin name for the genus that includes cherries, plums, peaches, apricots and almonds, among others; *subcordata* means somewhat heart-shaped and refers to its leaves. Klamath refers to the region in Oregon and California where it's most common; plum refers to its purple fruit. Also called Oregon or Sierra plum.

Compare with: cherries; apples and crabapples; buckthorns.

Form: Thicket-forming shrub or small tree reaching 40 feet tall and 8 inches in diameter.

Leaves: Simple, alternate, deciduous. Oblong to obovate; 2–4 inches long; margins serrated; apex pointed; petiole 1 inch; two to four prominent glands on base or petiole. Dark green to yellow-green above; paler below with occasional pubescence.

Flowers/fruit: Small (½-inch), fragrant, white flowers borne in elongated clusters 3–6 inches long. Fruits are red when young and purple or black when mature; ¼–½ inch in diameter; edible but bitter. Seeds contain cyanide and should not be swallowed in large numbers.

Twigs/bark: Twigs green-brown and smooth or pubescent when young; red-brown and smooth with age. Spur shoots common on older branches. Bark thin, broken and scaly. Lenticels not evident.

Range/habitat: Ranges across Canada and the northern United States. Occurs throughout most of the West in low to mid elevations in a variety of habitats.

Notes: Valuable browse for large mammals, including cattle and sheep, but can be poisonous in large quantities. Most animals eat its fruits. Raw fruits are bitter but prized for jam and jelly; Indigenous people use them in pemmican. Widely planted as an ornamental. Reproduces by seed and rhizomes. Fire may stimulate seed germination; sprouts readily after fire. Commonly affected by a fungus that causes large cankers on the trunk that eventually kill the plant.

Names: Rose family, *Rosaceae. Prunus* is the Latin name for the genus that includes cherries, plums, peaches, apricots and almonds, among others; *virginiana* recognizes its occurrence in Virginia. Chokecherry refers to the bitter taste of its fruits. Varieties include common, western and black chokecherry.

Compare with: other cherries; apples and crabapples; buckthorns.

Form: Upright, highly branched deciduous shrub; commonly 2–4 feet tall but sometimes 10–15 feet tall.

Leaves: Simple, alternate (commonly clustered at nodes and on spur shoots), deciduous (may persist under mild conditions). Small (¼–¾-inch); wedge-shaped; three-lobed apex (sometimes more). Margins entire and revolute; petiole short. Green to gray-green above; gray-white below. Hairy on both surfaces; not distinctly aromatic. Among the first plants to leaf out in spring and holds leaves until early winter.

Flowers/fruit: Small, yellow, tubular flowers with flared petals borne singly in leaf axils. Fruits are single or paired achenes; ¼–½ inch long; elliptical or tear-shaped with tapered tip or beak; bitter.

Twigs/bark: Young twigs slender; red-brown turning gray-red-brown with age. Smooth, bitter. Spur shoots common. Bark thin and gray-brown.

Range/habitat: Common at low to mid elevations (200–9,000 feet) across the dry Intermountain West. Grows on dry soils in the understory of ponderosa pine forests, commonly with sagebrush. Shade intolerant.

Notes: Important winter browse for elk, deer, antelope and domestic livestock. Deer, sheep, cattle and small mammals eat its seeds; rodents and ants are important seed dispersers. Used extensively in restoration projects. May fix nitrogen under some conditions. Reproduces by seed, layering and sprouting. Hybridizes with other bitterbrush species. Highly flammable; keep it away from homes and other structures. Fire commonly kills plants.

Names: Rose family, *Rosaceae*. *Purshia* honors Fredrick Pursh, a German botanist who worked in North America; *tridentata* refers to three-toothed leaf apex. Also called antelope bitterbrush and antelope bush.

Compare with: sagebrush, rabbitbrush, other bitterbrush species.

Form: Erect evergreen shrub; occasionally a small tree. Typically less than 15 feet tall.

Leaves: Simple, alternate, persistent. Ovate to elliptical; 1–4 inches long. Prominent parallel lateral veins (underside); margins entire or serrated, often rolled under. Thick in sun; thinner in shade; dark green above; paler below. Both surfaces glabrous except for rusty hairs on midrib and petiole.

Flowers/fruit: Small (⅛–¼-inch), green-white flowers borne in small, loose clusters in leaf axils. Fruits are round, purple to black drupes; ¼ inch in diameter; typically two seeds per drupe.

Twigs/bark: Young twigs slender to moderately stout; red-brown and pubescent turning dark red-brown and smooth, then gray. Winter buds naked with obvious veins and brown pubescence. Bark thin; gray-brown and mottled with chalky-white patches of lichens.

Range/habitat: Range limited to southwestern Oregon and western California. Most common on dry, shallow, stony sites in full sun but also occurs on moist slopes and ravines. Common component of California chaparral and oak woodlands; less frequent in coniferous forests.

Notes: Twigs and bark are bitter; many animals eat the twigs and fruits. Its bark is sometimes used as a laxative, but not to the same extent as that of cascara buckthorn. Its fruits resemble coffee beans but are not a useful substitute. Indigenous people eat the fruits and use them in various medicines. Reproduces by seed and basal sprouting, both with and without fire.

Names: Buckthorn family, *Rhamnaceae*. In Greek, *Rhamnus* refers to a thorny shrub; *californica* refers to its predominant home range. Also called California or Sierra coffeeberry. Some classify the genus as *Frangula*.

Compare with: Cascara buckthorn, cherries.

Form: Erect shrub or small tree to 50 feet tall and 20 inches in diameter.

Leaves: Simple, alternate, deciduous. Oblong; 2–6 inches long; prominently penniveined (very noticeable on underside); margins entire, finely serrated, or wavy (often on same plant). Thin to thick; dark green above; paler below, often with golden brown hairs along midrib.

Flowers/fruit: Small (⅛–¼-inch), green-white flowers borne in small, loose clusters in leaf axils. Fruits are round, purple to black drupes; ⅓ inch in diameter. Fruits have yellow pulp and are not edible (a natural laxative).

Twigs/bark: Young twigs slender to moderately stout; red-brown and pubescent turning dark red-brown and smooth, then gray. Winter buds naked with obvious veins and brown pubescence. Bark thin, gray-brown and mottled with chalky-white patches of lichens. Inner bark yellow.

Range/habitat: Ranges from British Columbia to southern California and into western Montana. Most common west of the Cascades in low to midelevation coniferous forests. Grows on moist, well-drained sites, especially along streams. Very shade tolerant.

Notes: Cured bark is a natural laxative and one of the most important natural drug products in North America; Indigenous people also use it for this purpose. Vigorous stump sprouter; stripping the bark causes sprouting, but stripped trees should be felled to better stimulate sprouting. Sprouts after fire. Birds and mammals eat its fruits; browsers nip the twigs. Bark and berries are used to make yellow dye.

Names: Buckthorn family, *Rhamnaceae*. In Greek, *Rhamnus* refers to a thorny shrub; *purshiana* honors Fredrick Pursh, a German botanist who worked in North America. Cascara is derived from the Spanish word for bark. Commonly called chittam or chittim, especially by those who work in the woods; sometimes called bearberry or coffee-tree. Some classify the genus as *Frangula*.

Compare with: California buckthorn, cherries.

Form: Erect, slender-branched deciduous shrub to 8 feet tall.

Leaves: Simple, alternate, deciduous; typically clustered along branches and near branch tips. Elliptical to oblong; 1½–4 inches long; margins entire but often wavy or wrinkled; end of middle vein does not form a nipple at apex (compare with *Menziesia*). Upper surface yellow-green with fine, rusty hairs; crinkled; not sticky; turn beautiful red, orange or bronze in fall.

Flowers/fruit: Large (½–1-inch), showy, white or cream-colored, cup-shaped flowers borne in clusters of two to four on previous year's growth. Fruits are small (about ¼-inch long), brown capsules; occur in clusters.

Twigs/bark: Young twigs covered in fine, red hairs. Mature bark gray; smooth to peeling.

Range/habitat: Grows in moist, subalpine coniferous forests and meadows. Common along streams and in wet meadows but also occurs on drier sites. Often found on glacial and colluvial deposits.

Notes: Not often browsed. Leaves of most rhododendrons are poisonous to many mammals. However, some Indigenous people use its leaves for tea and its buds to treat colds and sore throats and as a poultice to treat wounds. Reproduces by seed, rhizomes and layering.

Names: Heath family, *Ericaceae*. *Rhododendron* means rose tree; *albiflorum* refers to its white flowers. Also called white rhododendron, white-flowered rhododendron and mountain misery (because it grows in dense tangles).

Compare with: Pacific rhododendron, western azalea, rusty menziesia (false azalea), black twinberry, Indian-plum.

Form: Large evergreen shrub to 12 feet tall. Dense in sun but gangly in shade.

Leaves: Simple, alternate, persistent; most are clustered near branch tips. Elliptical to oblong; 3–6 inches long. Margins entire and often slightly revolute; apex and base acute. Petiole about 1 inch, stout. Thick and leathery. Dark green and smooth above; paler green and sometimes rusty below.

Flowers/fruit: Large (1–2 inches long), showy, white to rose-purple, bell-shaped flowers borne in large, loose clusters. Fruits are small (about ½-inch long), brown, hairy, five-parted capsules; occur in clusters. Seeds are tiny.

Twigs/bark: Young twigs stout; glabrous; green turning red-brown or gray. Buds large (especially terminal flower buds), green, and pointed with numerous imbricate scales. Bark gray-brown; thin; smooth or scale.

Range/habitat: Prefers moist but well-drained to dry sites in sun or shade; sea level to 4,500 feet. Prefers forest edges and can tolerate sites low in productivity, light and nutrients.

Notes: One of our most spectacular flowering plants. State flower of Washington. *Rhododendron* genus contains more than 1,000 species worldwide. Poisonous to sheep but eaten by mountain beavers. Thickets provide good thermal and hiding cover for animals and help control erosion. Its shallow root system makes it vulnerable to fire damage, but it sprouts after fire or cutting. Often indicates low soil nitrogen. Mycorrhizal association may facilitate nutrient uptake.

Names: Heath family, *Ericaceae*. *Rhododendron* means rose tree; *macrophyllum* means big leaf. Also called California rosebay, California rhododendron and coast rhododendron.

Compare with: Pacific madrone, western azalea, Cascade azalea.

Form: Loosely branched deciduous shrub to 10 feet tall.

Leaves: Simple, alternate, deciduous. Elliptical to obovate; 2–4 inches long; margins entire but often wavy and have distinct individual hairs; apex and base acute; petiole short (½ inch). Green and smooth above; paler green below, sometimes with sparse hairs.

Flowers/fruit: Showy, trumpet-shaped flowers borne in loose clusters. White to pink flowers, often tinged with yellow; 1–2 inches long. Fruits are small (about ½-inch long), brown, pubescent, five-parted capsules, occurring in clusters.

Twigs/bark: Young twigs slender, red- to orange-brown and finely pubescent. Older twigs gray-brown and smooth. Buds small (about ¼ inch) with red, imbricate scales. Bark gray-brown, thin, smooth or scaly.

Range/habitat: One of two deciduous rhododendrons native to western North America (the other is *R. albiflorum*). Ranges from southwestern Oregon to southern California. Grows on moist, but not wet, sites in sun or shade. Some report it growing in peaty bogs. Can grow on serpentine soils.

Notes: Poisonous to livestock. Common ornamental. One of the few fragrant rhododendrons.

Names: Heath family, *Ericaceae*. *Rhododendron* means rose tree; *occidentale* means western. Most deciduous members of the *Rhodendron* genus are called azaleas.

Compare with: Pacific rhododendron, Cascade azalea, black twinberry, Indian-plum, rusty menziesia (false azalea).

Form: Erect, unarmed deciduous shrub; 3–10 feet tall.

Leaves: Simple, alternate, deciduous; smaller leaves often clustered on spur shoots. Small (¼–2 inches); three rounded lobes (sometimes five); nearly round. Green and semiglossy above; paler green below. No pubescence.

Flowers/fruit: Small, bright yellow flowers borne in erect or dropping clusters of five to 15; fragrance sometimes described as cloves or vanilla. Fruits are small (¼- to ½-inch) berries; amber to red to black.

Twigs/bark: Twigs and stems round; unarmed; red-brown and smooth or covered in tiny hairs when young. Spur shoots common. Bark yellow-brown to red-brown darkening with age; prominent lenticels.

Range/habitat: Native to western North America but naturalized elsewhere; in Oregon and Washington, occurs east of the Cascade crest. Wide ecological amplitude; grows in riparian and upland areas to 8,000 feet. Common near water but drought tolerant.

Notes: Variable browse value; birds and small mammals eat its fruits. Alternate host for white pine blister rust, which kills five-needled pines. Reproduces by basal sprouts and rhizomes. Seeds are distributed by animals and stored in soil banks. Hot fires are likely to destroy plants and seed banks; low and moderate fires stimulate sprouting. Early to midsuccessional species. Cultivated as an ornamental. Its fruits are used in jam and jelly; the dried, pulverized inner bark is used in traditional medicines.

Names: Currant family, *Grossulariaceae*. *Ribes* is from an Arabic word for a similar plant with acidic fruit; *aureum* refers to its golden flowers. Also called fragrant golden currant and buffalo currant.

Compare with: other currants and gooseberries, ninebark.

Form: Erect, unarmed deciduous shrub to 10 feet tall. Catty or skunky odor.

Leaves: Simple, alternate, deciduous. Large (2–10 inches wide); palmately lobed (maple-like); five to seven pointed lobes with deep sinuses; petiole typically longer than leaf blade, often with long hairs near base. Green and glabrous above; dull green below with sparse hairs and yellow glands that exude resin drops and a distinctive odor. Leaves stink when crushed. New leaves unfold in accordion fashion.

Flowers/fruit: Small, white to green-white flowers borne in long (5–12 inches), erect clusters of 20–40. Fruits are small, blue-black berries with whitish bloom. Fruits occur in long (5–12 inches) clusters. Edible, but taste is variable. Long clusters are distinctive since most currants bear fruit in small clumps.

Twigs/bark: Twigs and stems round; unarmed; heart-shaped leaf scars. Bark has yellow glands that smell sweet, skunky or catty. Older bark dark gray or brown.

Range/habitat: Grows mostly west of the Cascade crest but sometimes east in low to subalpine elevations. Inhabits moist to wet places.

Notes: Indigenous people eat its fruits fresh, dried or boiled, but Scottish botanist and plant explorer David Douglas reported that even a few berries caused vomiting. If eaten in large quantities, the fruits may cause nausea, cramping or constipation.

Names: Currant family, *Grossulariaceae*. *Ribes* is from an Arabic word for a similar plant with acidic fruit; *bracteosum* refers to the distinctive bracts on flower stalks. Also called stinking currant and stinking black currant.

Compare with: other currants and gooseberries, thimbleberry, devilsclub, ninebark.

Form: Erect, highly branched, unarmed deciduous shrub to 6 feet tall.

Leaves: Simple, alternate, deciduous. Small (typically less than 1 inch in diameter). Palmately lobed and serrated, but lobes are often so shallow that leaves appear toothed but unlobed; nearly round. Upper surface somewhat white and often waxy or sticky.

Flowers/fruit: Small (¼-inch), green-white to pink, tubular flowers borne in drooping clusters of two to eight; conspicuous bracts are longer than flower stalks. Fruits are red to orange, translucent, pea-sized berries containing many seeds; typically dry and not palatable.

Twigs/bark: Young twigs covered in fine, sticky hairs. Young bark tan; splits and shreds but does not exfoliate. Older bark thin, smooth and red-gray.

Range/habitat: Grows mostly east of the Cascade crest from central British Columbia into New Mexico and Arizona. Prefers open, dry coniferous forests, rocky slopes and alpine shrub communities.

Notes: Roots help stabilize disturbed soils; plant provides cover for young conifers. Low browse value. Nectar is important for hummingbirds; many animals eat its berries. Fruits are used in jam, jelly and often pemmican. Reproduces mainly by seed; not rhizomatous. Seeds can remain dormant in the soil for many years. Fire typically kills plants but stimulates seed germination. An alternate host for white pine blister rust (like all *Ribes*).

Names: Currant family, *Grossulariaceae*. *Ribes* is from an Arabic word for a similar plant with acidic fruit; *cereum* is Latin and refers to its waxy leaves. Also called squaw currant, but this name is offensive to many and will be used less over time.

Compare with: ninebark, other currants and gooseberries.

Form: Spiny deciduous shrub; 3–10 feet tall; erect to spreading.

Leaves: Simple, alternate, deciduous. Palmately lobed and serrated; usually three lobes, sometimes five; generally 1–3 inches wide, sometimes larger; petiole long with distinctive hairs. Green above; paler green below; fine pubescence; no distinctive aroma (unusual for *Ribes*).

Flowers/fruit: Fuchsia-like flowers hang pendent in groups of one to four; green to red, reflexed calyx; white, skirt-like petals; stamens are numerous and longer than petals. Fruits are round, black berries less than ½ inch in diameter. Edible berries are among the best of the currants and gooseberries.

Twigs/bark: Young twigs green with one to three stout, chestnut-colored spines at most nodes. Older twigs tan; they often have numerous thin prickles between larger nodal spines. Thorniest of all the gooseberries. Gray-brown bark is armed with spines and prickles.

Range/habitat: Occurs at mid to low elevations from southern British Columbia through southern California; mostly west of the Cascades and Sierras (some exceptions). Prefers moist sites along streams, meadows and forest edges in full sun or partial shade.

Notes: Fruits are edible, cooked or raw. Indigenous people chew the inner bark to treat colds and sore throats, boil the roots and weave them into rope, and use the spines to lance boils and blisters. Pollinated by insects. An alternate host for white pine blister rust (like all *Ribes*). Found in plant collections of Lewis and Clark.

Names: Currant family, *Grossulariaceae*. *Ribes* is from an Arabic word for a similar plant with acidic fruit; *divaricatum* refers to its spreading form. Also called black and coastal black gooseberry because of its fruit color and straggly gooseberry because of its growth form.

Compare with: ninebark, thimbleberry, other currants and gooseberries.

Form: Spiny, spindly deciduous shrub; 3–6 feet tall; erect in sun but trailing in shade. Grows alone or in thickets.

Leaves: Simple, alternate, deciduous. 1–2½ inches in diameter; palmately lobed and serrated (maple-like); three to five lobes; deeply incised. Dark green above but not hairy or glandular; hairy below.

Flowers/fruit: Small, green to maroon, saucer-shaped flowers borne in drooping clusters of five to 15. Fruits are dark purple, pea-sized berries covered in stalked glands; fall from their stalks when ripe; edible, but taste is often weak.

Twigs/bark: Young twigs heavily armed at nodes with multipart spines; single prickles often occur between nodes. Older twigs mostly unarmed.

Range/habitat: Occurs at mid to high elevations across Canada and most northern U.S. states as far south as Colorado and Virginia. Most common in moist forests, especially near water. Moderately shade tolerant but prefers openings.

Notes: Some people are allergic to its prickles. Some Indigenous people harvest its berries and think the prickly stems have special protective powers. Moderate browse value; many animals eat its berries. Reproduces primarily by seed but sometimes by layering. Response to fire depends on severity. An alternate host for white pine blister rust (like all *Ribes*).

Names: Currant family, *Grossulariaceae*. *Ribes* is from an Arabic word for a similar plant with acidic fruit; *lacustre* refers to its tendency to grow near lakes. Also called swamp currant, black gooseberry, black swamp gooseberry and bristly black currant. Prickly refers to armed stems; swamp refers to locations where it's commonly found.

Compare with: ninebark, thimbleberry, other currants and gooseberries.

Form: Spiny deciduous shrub; 2–5 feet tall; erect in sun but trailing in shade. Grows alone or in thickets.

Leaves: Simple, alternate, deciduous; often clustered at nodes. Small (less than 1 inch in diameter); palmately lobed; three to five toothed lobes; nearly round. Hairless to hairy; no sticky glands below.

Flowers/fruit: Spectacular small (½-inch), pendulous flowers borne singly or in clusters of two to three. Red to purple sepals with five white petals. Fruits are large (½-inch), red to purple berries covered in sharp spines and gland-tipped bristles; edible (once you get past the spines).

Twigs/bark: Young twigs heavily armed at nodes with tri-parted spines; no prickles between nodes; distinctly red with red spines. Mature bark gray-brown; often spits to reveal lenticels.

Range/habitat: Found primarily in California and southwest Oregon but has been spotted on Tombstone Pass farther north. Common in chaparral communities, oak woodlands and dry coniferous forests.

Notes: Browsed by many species, but value seems low. Animals and water spread its seeds, which can be stored in the soil for long periods. Top-killed by fire but may resprout if damage is not too severe. Pioneer species that thrives after logging and fire. Humans eat its fruits raw, dried, or in jam and jelly. Flowers herald spring in the Sierra foothills and attract hummingbirds and butterflies. An alternate host for white pine blister rust (like all *Ribes*).

Names: Currant family, *Grossulariaceae*. *Ribes* is from an Arabic word for a similar plant with acidic fruit; *roezlii* honors Benedict Roezl, a Czech botanist who worked in Latin America. Sierra refers to its primary habitat; gooseberry refers to most spined members of the *Ribes* genus. Also called shiny-leaved gooseberry.

Compare with: other currants and gooseberries.

Form: Erect, loosely branched, unarmed deciduous shrub; commonly 3–10 feet tall.

Leaves: Simple, alternate, deciduous. 1–4 inches in diameter; palmately lobed and serrated (maple-like). Three to five usually rounded lobes. Petiole 1–1½ inches, glandular and pubescent. Dark green and pubescent above; paler green and velvety below.

Flowers/fruit: Small (¼-inch), pink to red, tubular flowers borne in long, showy, drooping racemes. Flowers and leaves emerge together. Fruits are dark blue, pea-sized berries covered in stalked glands and white, waxy bloom. Edible but often bitter and unpalatable.

Twigs/bark: Young twigs round; green and pubescent turning red-brown and smooth with age. Bark thin; red- to gray-brown; splits longitudinally to reveal vertical rows of horizontal lenticels.

Range/habitat: Grows on dry to moist, well-drained sites in sun or shade at low to mid elevations. Prefers sunny habitats.

Notes: Glands on leaves and fruits have a distinctive odor. Flowers are a favorite of hummingbirds. Common ornamental; flowers on cultivated plants range from white to dark red. One of several dozen western species of *Ribes* in western North America; all are alternate hosts for white pine blister rust. It is said that David Douglas, a Scottish botanist and plant explorer, helped finance his collecting trips to North America by selling seeds of this plant.

Names: Currant family, *Grossulariaceae*. *Ribes* is from an Arabic word for a similar plant with acidic fruit; *sanguineum* means bloodred and refers to its flower color.

Compare with: ninebark, thimbleberry, other currants.

Form: Erect to spreading, unarmed deciduous shrub 3–6 feet tall; straggly or stiff and bushy.

Leaves: Simple, alternate, deciduous. 1–3 inches wide; palmately lobed (three to five lobes); margins toothed. Both surfaces covered in soft, sticky hairs. Very aromatic. Similar to *R. sanguineum* except for additional stickiness.

Flowers/fruit: Small (¼–½ inches long), green-white to pink, bell-shaped flowers borne in erect to drooping clusters of three to 12; green flower stalk bracts are shorter than flowers. Fruits are round, blue-black berries without bloom; very sticky. Reports of edibility vary.

Twigs/bark: Stems round, unarmed. Young twigs green and hairy turning tan to red-brown with exfoliating bark and orange lenticels. Mature bark gray-brown with rows of lenticels.

Range/habitat: Distribution is scattered, but it may be common locally. Most common in mid to subalpine elevations east of the Cascades. Grows in moist to dry conditions in open and forested sites, commonly with sagebrush.

Notes: Many currants have sticky leaves, but these are the stickiest. Emits a strong odor in hot weather. One report lists fruits as an "esteemed" part of Montana Indians' diet, but others report variable usage. An alternate host for white pine blister rust (like all *Ribes*).

Names: Currant family, *Grossulariaceae*. *Ribes* is from an Arabic word for a similar plant with acidic fruit; *viscosus* means sticky in Latin and refers to the glandular hairs that cover most plant parts. Currant is derived from "raisin of Corinth" and refers to small, dried grapes used in baking. Also called sticky flowering currant.

Compare with: other currants (especially red-flowering), thimbleberry, ninebark.

***R. nutkana*, Nootka rose**

Overview: A large, diverse genus with many species and thousands of hybrids and cultivars. Often cultivated for their beautiful, aromatic flowers. Distinctions between wild roses are often subtle; many species hybridize, mixing characteristics and making identification difficult. This section describes general characteristics of wild roses and briefly describes several common Pacific Northwest species.

Form: Most are erect shrubs, but some climb or trail. Commonly intertwined with other plants.

Leaves: Pinnately compound (usually five to nine leaflets), alternate, deciduous. All have stipules (leafy "ears") where the petiole joins the stem; most have prickles on veins. Leaflets more or less oval. Margins are distinctly serrated or doubly serrated.

Flowers/fruit: Flowers of all Pacific Northwest roses are pink, although some naturalized species are white. Flowers have five petals; some occur singly while others are clustered. Edible, orange to red fruits, known as hips, occur singly or in clusters depending on species; many are known for high levels of vitamin C.

Twigs/bark: Twigs slender to stout; always armed with prickles (commonly called thorns, but they are not). Prickles vary from slender to stout and straight to hooked. Prickles are numerous to sparse; density may vary on the same stem. Mature bark often red to gray.

Range/habitat: Roses grow in a variety of habitats. East of the Cascades, they are common along streams; west of the Cascades, they occur almost anywhere.

Notes: Native roses are not common ornamentals, but they beautify forests and smell heavenly. Rose hips can be brewed into tea and made into jam and jelly; birds and mammals also enjoy them. Roses are used to make perfumes and flavoring agents and are commonly celebrated in symbolism and verse.

Names: Rose family, *Rosaceae*.

Pacific Northwest roses

The Pacific Northwest has 10–12 species that are native or naturalized.

***R. canina*, dog rose:** five to seven leaflets; broadly elliptical to nearly round; serrated with glandular teeth. Flowers white to pink; usually solitary. Fruits bright red; up to 1 inch long. Stout, flat, hooked prickles. Introduced from Eurasia; widespread but scattered on both sides of the Cascades.

***R. eglanteria*, sweetbriar rose:** five to seven leaflets; ovate to elliptical; coarsely toothed with glandular teeth. Flowers clear pink. Fruits urn-shaped; up to ½ inch long. Stout, flat, hooked prickles. Nonnative but naturalized across North America; widespread west of the Cascades; less common to the east.

***R. gymnocarpa*, little wood rose:** Plant is spindly. five to nine leaflets; elliptical to ovate; doubly serrated with glandular tips. Flowers pink to rose; usually singular. Fruits orange to scarlet; pear-shaped. Calyx deciduous as fruit matures. Numerous straight, slender prickles. Native, widespread and common.

***R. multiflora*, multiflora rose:** Largest of the wild roses. Five to nine leaflets; oblong to obovate; 1–2 inches long; sharply serrated. Stipules resemble fused hairs. Flowers white, single or clustered. Fruits orange to red; calyx persistent; hairy seeds inside. Broad-based, straight or curved prickles; paired at nodes but single and smaller between. Introduced from Japan. Highly invasive.

PHOTO: NATURESERVE, CC BY 2.0

***R. nutkana*, Nootka rose:** five to nine leaflets; ovate to elliptical with coarse, glandular teeth. Large, pink flowers usually single but sometimes clustered. Fruits red to purple; pear-shaped; calyx persistent. Paired, straight prickles at each leaf base with a few prickles between nodes. Native; widespread west of the Cascades and less common to the east.

PHOTO: LESLIE SEATON, CC BY 2.0

***R. pisocarpa*: clustered rose:** five to seven leaflets; sharply pointed and serrated; not glandular. Flowers small, deep pink and clustered. Fruits round to elongated; clustered; calyx persistent. Paired prickles below each leaf node. Widespread west of the Cascades; less common to the east.

PHOTO: JOHN RUSK, CC BY 2.0

***R. woodsii*, Wood's rose:** five to seven leaflets; oblong; coarse, singly serrated; not glandular. Flowers pink with broad petals; clustered. Fruits red; round to elongated; less than ½ inch long; clustered; calyx persistent. Paired, straight prickles at each leaf node with many smaller prickles between nodes. Widespread in western North America; more common east of the Cascades than west.

PHOTO: JAMES ST. JOHN, CC BY 2.0

Form: Erect, spreading, or trailing evergreen shrub to 30 feet long. Grows in dense, impenetrable thickets. Young, erect stems arch as they lengthen, eventually touching the ground and rooting.

Leaves: Palmately compound (usually five leaflets), alternate, persistent (often barely so). Leaflets oval; 1½–3 inches long (sometimes larger); margins serrated; rachis and petiole armed with heavy, recurved prickles. Dark green above; heavy, white bloom below.

Flowers/fruit: Large (about 1-inch), white (most commonly) to pink flowers borne in clusters of five to 20. Fruits are tasty aggregates of small, black drupelets; about 1 inch long. When picked, "berry" adheres to torus (central core).

Twigs/bark: Stout; heavily ribbed; purple-red; armed with heavy, recurved prickles. Stems biennial. First-year stems sterile; second-year stems bear fruit.

Range/habitat: Native to Asia; introduced to North America from England for berry production but soon escaped cultivation. Now grows widely on a variety of sites across North America. Commonly regarded as a serious pest despite tasty berries. Highly invasive.

Notes: Widely used in jam and jelly but often considered less tasty than native blackberries. Birds and mammals eat its fruits and use the tangled thickets for cover. Browsed by many species despite its thorny nature. Reproduces by seed and aggressive vegetative means. Roots at nodes; sprouts after fire.

Names: Rose family, *Rosaceae*. *Rubus* is Latin for red and for brambles; *discolor* means two-colored, probably in reference to its leaves. Also called Himalaya blackberry and Himalaya berry. Some categorize it as *R. bifrons*, *R. armeniacus* or *R. ulmifolius*.

Compare with: other blackberries, salmonberry, thimbleberry.

Form: Erect or arching evergreen shrub that gets very large. Grows in dense, impenetrable, thorny thickets. Young, erect stems arch as they lengthen, eventually touching the ground and rooting.

Leaves: Palmately compound (usually five deeply lacerated leaflets), alternate, persistent. Rachis and petiole heavily armed with stout, recurved prickles. Green to green-red above; paler green below.

Flowers/fruit: Large (about 1 inch), white to pink flowers borne in clusters. Fruits are aggregates of small, black drupelets; about 1 inch long; very tasty. When picked, "berry" adheres to torus (central core).

Twigs/bark: Stout; heavily ribbed; purple-red (may be green underneath. Armed with stout, recurved prickles. Stems biennial. First-year stems sterile; second-year stems bear fruit.

Habitat/Range: Native to Eurasia but widely naturalized in North America. Introduced to North America for berry production but escaped cultivation. Common on barren, infertile and disturbed sites (logged or burned); along roads and in abandoned fields. Requires good moisture for growth. Highly invasive.

Notes: Widely used in jam and jelly. Birds and mammals eat its fruits and use the tangled thickets for cover. Reproduces by seed and aggressive vegetative means; fire stimulates germination of seeds stored in the soil. Sprouts readily from root crowns, rhizomes and layered branch tips. There are many cultivated varieties, including thornless.

Names: Rose family, *Rosaceae*. *Rubus* is Latin for red and for brambles; *laciniatus* means divided into narrow lobes. Evergreen refers to its evergreen nature, but several other blackberries are also evergreen. Also called cutleaf blackberry because of its lacerated leaflets.

Compare with: other blackberries and raspberries, salmonberry, thimbleberry.

Form: Deciduous shrub with arching habit to 6 feet tall. Commonly forms thorny thickets.

Leaves: Compound (usually three or five leaflets), alternate, deciduous. Leaflets broadly ovate and coarsely toothed. Stems, petioles, and leaf veins commonly armed with flattened, hooked prickles. Green and crinkly above, pale green or white below. Covered in soft hairs.

Flowers/fruit: Small (to 1 inch), white to pink flowers borne terminally or in leaf axils; single or clusters of three to seven. Fruits are aggregates of drupelets; about ½ inch in diameter. They are initially red but darken to purple or black, covered in whitish bloom. Tasty fruit is distinctly hairy. When picked, torus (the center core) stays attached to plant, leaving a thimblelike "berry."

Twigs/bark: Round; covered in white bloom; armed with curved, flattened prickles. Stems biennial. First-year stems sterile; second-year stems bear fruit.

Range/habitat: Native. Grows throughout the Pacific Northwest into the Southwest; 0–7,000 feet. Prefers moist, well-drained soils but tolerates many soil types. Typically found in open, disturbed sites, especially burned clear-cuts and open forests. Commonly grows with wild blackberry, *R. ursinus*, which it closely resembles.

Notes: Wildlife and humans readily eat black raspberries. Indigenous people use its fruits as a key ingredient in stain mixtures and use infusions of leaves and roots to treat a variety of digestive ailments.

Names: Rose family, *Rosaceae*. *Rubus* is Latin for red and for brambles; *leucodermis* means white skinned and refers to its bark. Black refers to its fruit. Also called blackcap, western raspberry, western black raspberry and whitebark raspberry.

Compare with: other blackberries (especially *R. ursinus*) and raspberries.

Form: Erect, spindly, unarmed deciduous shrub, commonly 3–6 feet tall. Often forms dense thickets.

Leaves: Simple, alternate, deciduous. Large (3–10 inches in diameter); palmately lobed and serrated. Three to seven (usually five) broad lobes. Dark green and velvety on both surfaces, with glandular hairs.

Flowers/fruit: Large (1-inch) flowers borne terminally; single or small clusters; broad, white petals feel like crinkled tissue paper. Fruits are aggregates of red drupelets in the shape of a flattened dome with sparse, long hairs. Fruits are edible but often dry; flavor varies. When picked, torus (the central core) stays attached to plant, leaving a thimblelike "berry" that falls apart easily.

Twigs/bark: New stems green, hairy and glandular. Older stems (canes) are light brown, round and unarmed. Bark on older canes is thin, tan and papery. Stems usually live several years; first-year stems are sterile; older stems bear fruit.

Range/habitat: Native. Widely distributed on moist, sunny sites from the Great Lakes to the Pacific Ocean and from Alaska to Mexico; 0–9,000 feet. Moderately shade tolerant but prefers open, disturbed sites to shady forests.

Notes: Fruits are edible but seldom gathered in large quantities. Indigenous people harvest and dry its berries and eat the young shoots. Birds and mammals enjoy its fruits, which are of variable browse value. Reproduces by seed and underground rhizomes. Seeds can remain viable in the soil for many years.

Names: Rose family, *Rosaceae*. *Rubus* is Latin for red and for brambles; *parviflorus* refers to little flowers, but this seems odd since thimbleberry flowers are larger than other *Rubus* flowers. Thimbleberry refers to the shape of the picked fruit. Also called western thimbleberry.

Compare with: salmonberry, stink currant, other blackberries and raspberries.

Form: Erect, spindly deciduous shrub; armed with numerous fine prickles; commonly 3–15 feet tall. Forms dense thickets in sun.

Leaves: Compound (three leaflets), alternate, deciduous. Leaflets ovate; 1–3 inches long; margins doubly serrated or lobed and serrated; opposing lateral leaflets often resemble a butterfly. Green above and below; wrinkled surface above; armed below.

Flowers/fruit: Large (1–1½-inches), bright pink to dark red flowers borne singly or in clusters of two to four. Fruits are aggregates of small, yellow to red (often salmon) drupelets; similar to a mushy raspberry; taste varies. When picked, torus (the central core) stays attached to the plant, leaving a thimblelike "berry."

Twigs/bark: New stems green, armed. Bark on older stems is orange, papery thin and exfoliating. It's covered in fine prickles that detach easily. Stems are biennial. First-year stems are sterile; second-year stems bear fruit.

Range/habitat: Native. Range includes most of the West Coast into Idaho, from sea level to subalpine. Widely distributed on wet sites in sun or shade. Especially common on disturbed sites along streams and avalanche tracks.

Notes: Indigenous people harvest its berries and eat the young shoots. Many animals browse its foliage and eat the berries. Seldom browsed by cattle or sheep. Hummingbirds enjoy nectar from its flowers. Reproduces primarily by underground rhizomes, often forming dense, impenetrable thickets above and below ground. Early leaf out helps it survive in heavy shade. Often impedes reforestation.

Names: Rose family, *Rosaceae*. *Rubus* is Latin for red and for brambles; *spectabilis* means spectacular and may refer to its flowers. Salmonberry refers to its fruit color. One of the few shrubs with only one common name.

Compare with: other blackberries and raspberries.

Form: Trailing or climbing evergreen shrub to 20 feet long. Grows alone and in dense tangles; armed.

Leaves: Pinnately compound (usually three leaflets but sometimes five), alternate, persistent (but barely so). Leaflets ovate; 1½–3 inches long; lobed and doubly serrated. The rachis and petiole are armed with slender, easily detached prickles. Dark green above; paler below.

Flowers/fruit: Large (1-inch), white to pink flowers with narrow petals borne in clusters. Imperfect, with males and females on separate plants. Fruits are aggregates of black drupelets, ½ inch long and very tasty. When picked, "berry" adheres to torus (the central core).

Twigs/bark: Round, slender, green to red and darkening with age. Covered in white, waxy bloom. Armed with slender, straight or recurved prickles that detach easily. Stems are biennial. First-year stems sterile; second-year stems bear fruit.

Range/habitat: Native. Range stretches south into Mexico and east into Idaho. Occurs in open woods and newly disturbed areas in many different plant communities.

Notes: Excellent flavor; widely used in jam and jelly. Several commercial blackberries are derived from this species. Birds and mammals eat its fruits and use the tangled thickets for cover; deer and elk browse its leaves and stems. Indigenous people eat its fruits fresh, dry fruits into cakes for winter use, and brew tea with the berries and leaves. Reproduces easily by seed and aggressive sprouting, suckering and rooting. Rapidly colonizes burned and logged sites because it roots at nodes of trailing stems.

Names: Rose family, *Rosaceae*. *Rubus* is Latin for red and for brambles; *ursinus* refers to bears, which enjoy its fruits. Also called trailing blackberry, California blackberry and western dewberry, among many others.

Compare with: other blackberries and raspberries.

Overview: A large, diverse genus with many species — perhaps 400 worldwide, 135 in North America, and 60 in the Pacific Northwest. Distinctions between willows are often subtle; many species hybridize, mixing characteristics and making identification difficult. This section describes general characteristics of willows and briefly describes several common Pacific Northwest species.

Form: Some grow as trees; most are shrubby with multiple stems. Many shrubby species are large, exceeding 20 feet tall with stems 6–12 inches in diameter; others are shorter or prostrate.

Leaves: Simple, alternate, and deciduous. Most are long and narrow (elliptical to lanceolate), but some are oval to nearly round. Margins range from entire to wavy, to distinctly serrated with rounded teeth. All leaves have short petioles (leaf stems). Nearly all have stipules (leafy ears) where the petiole joins its twig. Some stipules last most or all of the growing season while some drop sooner.

Flowers/fruit: Male and female flowers are borne in single sex catkins (aments), almost always on separate plants. Most willows flower and fruit in the spring, but some do so in the fall. When spring-flowering, flowers typically appear before the leaves. Catkins may hang or be erect. Fruits are small capsules containing numerous cottony seeds that are distributed by wind and water. Seeds are tiny and need to land on moist sites to survive germination. Most male flowers first appear as smooth, soft "pussy willows."

Twigs/bark: Twigs slender to stout, often brittle and easily broken from larger branches. They are smooth to densely wooly; red, orange, yellow, green or brown. Terminal buds are absent; lateral buds are typically appressed to twig. Buds typically covered with a single, cap-like scale; some species have overlapping scales. Pith is round and uniform. Bark is variable but typically gray, smooth to scaly. Wood high in moisture.

Range/habitat: Willows range from the Tropics to the Arctic; from sea level to tree line. They are commonly associated with water (flowing or standing). Most prefer moist soil in the full sun.

Notes: Leaves and twigs are browsed by large mammals (deer, moose and elk), and are a favorite of beavers. Inner bark can be dried, ground into powder and added to flour for use in bread. Bark contains salicin (a key ingredient in aspirin) and high levels of auxin (used to stimulate root production). Fibrous, tough, spreading roots help control erosion. Some species are important for honey production. Supple branches are woven into baskets, fish traps, furniture and snowshoes. Wood is used in brooms, cricket bats, polo balls, furniture, toys and turnery items.

Pacific Northwest willows

Of approximately 60 species in the Pacific Northwest, about 40 occur in Oregon, 40 in Washington, and 50 in British Columbia. Many are difficult to distinguish from other willows.

Cottony seeds spring from the female catkin of Lemmon's willow.

Male catkin of Scouler's willow in both "pussy willow" and flowering stage.

The bark of Sitka willow is quite variable, but often smooth and greenish-yellow.

Names: Willow family, *Salicaeae*. *Salix* means to leap. Pennsylvania and Iowa have towns named Salix.

***S. bebbiana,* Bebb's willow:** Shrub/small tree. Leaves elliptical to obovate; margins smooth to coarsely toothed; sparsely hairy on both sides. Twigs densely hairy. Wet areas at mid to low elevations; primarily east of the Cascade crest. Common source of diamond willow.

***S. geyeriana,* Geyer's willow:** Erect shrub to 15 feet tall. Leaves 1–3 inches long; lanceolate to oblanceolate; margins nearly entire. Catkins appear before or with leaves. Wet meadows and streams; both sides of the Cascades.

***S. hookeriana,* Hooker's willow:** Large shrub/small tree. Leaves 2–5 inches long; oval to ovate; very hairy when young; stipules fall off early. Sand dunes; near water; low elevations; primarily west of the Cascade crest.

***S. lasiandra,* Pacific willow:** Slender shrub/small tree. Leaves 2–6 inches long; lanceolate; margins finely toothed; white bloom below. Yellow catkins. Wet areas; sea level to mid elevations; both sides of the Cascades.

***S. lemmonii,* Lemmon's willow:** Shrub to 15 feet tall. Leaves 2–4 inches long; elliptical to lanceolate; margins entire or inconspicuously toothed; shiny green above; pale glaucous below. Catkins appear before or with leaves. Riparian areas; primarily east of the Cascade crest.

***S. prolixa,* McKenzie willow:** Shrub. Leaves 2–6 inches long; lanceolate to ovate; apex acuminate; margins serrated. Catkins appear with leaves. Along streams; both sides of the Cascades.

***S. scouleriana,* Scouler's willow:** Tall shrub/small tree. Leaves 1–3 inches long; widest above midpoint; densely hairy when young; margins smooth or with few rounded teeth. Twigs densely hairy. Wet areas; low to mid elevations; both sides of the Cascades.

***S. sitchensis,* Sitka willow:** Shrub/small tree. Leaves 1–4 inches long; widest above midpoint; tapering to base; margins smooth or with tiny teeth; satiny but not white below. Twigs densely velvety; brittle at base. Wet areas; low to mid elevations; primarily west of the Cascade crest.

Form: Large, upright shrub with multiple stems or small tree to 20 feet or taller.

Leaves: Pinnately compound (5–9 leaflets) with some leaves doubly compound, opposite, deciduous. Large (6–12 inches long); leaflets lanceolate; margins serrated; apex pointed. Dark green and smooth above; paler green below.

Flowers/fruit: Tiny, white flowers borne in large, upright, flat-topped clusters. Fruits are small (1/16–1/8-inch), dark blue to black, berrylike drupes often covered in white bloom. They occur in upright, flat-topped clusters and are mildly poisonous unless fully ripe or cooked.

Twigs/bark: Opposite buds, twigs and leaves. Twigs large in diameter; typically covered in waxy bloom. They break easily. Pith is large and spongy. New sprouts may grow 10–12 feet in one year. Bark gray-brown to black with prominent, raised lenticels.

Range/habitat: Black elderberry occurs in every U.S. state and southern Canada; it is also widespread in Eurasia. Blue elderberry occurs throughout western North America. Grows on moist, well-drained sites in sun. Common in riparian areas.

Notes: Sprouts easily from base, forming large clumps; seeds can be stored in the soil for nearly 20 years. Fruits are valuable to wildlife and humans. They are often used in jam, jelly, wine, brandy and liqueurs. Elderberry has many medicinal uses in traditional cultures. It is valuable for wildlife browse, nectar and hiding cover.

Names: Honeysuckle family, *Caprifoliaceae*. *Sambucus* refers to a stringed instrument made from elder wood; *nigra* means black; *cerulea* means dark blue. *S. nigra* grows around the world; our subspecies is called blue elder or blue elderberry and was once recognized as its own species, *S. cerulea*. Many common and scientific names are associated with blue elder.

Compare with: red elderberry, Oregon ash, mountain-ash.

Form: Large, upright shrub with multiple stems or small tree; commonly 8–20 feet tall.

Leaves: Pinnately compound (5–7 leaflets), opposite, deciduous. Large (6–12 inches long); leaflets lanceolate; margins serrated; apex pointed. Dark green and smooth above; paler green and pubescent below.

Flowers/fruit: Tiny, white flowers borne in large, upright, cone-shaped clusters; strong odor. Fruits are small (¹⁄₁₆–⅛-inch), berrylike drupes; usually red but black in one variety. They occur in upright, cone-shaped clusters. Fruits are toxic when raw but edible when cooked.

Twigs/bark: Opposite buds, twigs, and leaves. Twigs large in diameter; often covered in waxy bloom; break easily. Pith soft; large; spongy. New sprouts may grow 10–12 feet in one year. Bark soft; gray to dark red-brown; prominent, raised lenticels.

Range/habitat: Native and widespread in North America and Eurasia. Common, but seldom dominant, on moist to wet sites in sun or shade.

Notes: Sprouts easily from base and rhizomes, often forming large clumps; seeds are commonly stored in leaf litter and soil. Fruits are valuable to wildlife; animals are important seed dispersers. Fruits are toxic when raw; cook before eating. Vegetative parts also contain compounds toxic to humans; Indigenous people use this plant as a purgative. May hybridize with blue elderberry. Leaves, twigs and flowers often have a foul smell when crushed. Leaves may stipple or bleach when exposed to high levels of ozone.

Names: Honeysuckle family, *Caprifoliaceae*. *Sambucus* refers to a stringed instrument made from elder wood; *racemosa* refers to flowers arranged in racemes. Also called red elder, coast red elder, and redberry elder.

Compare with: other elderberries, Oregon ash, mountain-ash.

Form: Erect, but often sprawling, shrub to 10 feet tall.

Leaves: Simple, opposite, deciduous. Oval; 1–2½ inches long; margins entire. Thick and leathery (may appear persistent); dark green above; pale green to silvery below with prominent, rusty dots. Small, terminal leaflet pairs resemble praying hands.

Flowers/fruit: Small, inconspicuous, yellow-brown flowers borne singly or in small clusters; usually dioecious. Fruits are small (¼-inch), red, translucent, oval berries. They are edible but bitter unless processed. Don't eat them raw because fruits contain a small amount of toxin (saponin) that breaks down with cooking.

Twigs/bark: Opposite buds and twigs. Young twigs are brown, covered in rusty brown dots or scales. Buds clasp twigs. Bark red-brown with prominent lenticels.

Range/habitat: Widespread across Canada, northern states and the Rockies. Occurs on well-drained, sandy or rocky sites and along riverbanks and roads. Prefers full sun or light shade.

Notes: Common on disturbed sites because it fixes nitrogen. Modest to low browse value; bears and grouse eat its fruits. Indigenous people use its fruits in many ways: pressed into cakes; beaten with other fruits to make a frothy dessert; and used in infusions and decoctions to treat a variety of conditions, including digestive and respiratory ailments, childbirth and arthritis, as well as to dye and curl hair. Reproduces by seed; sprouts from root crown and taproot.

Names: Oleaster family, *Eleagnaceae. Shepherdia* honors John Shepherd, the first curator of the Liverpool Botanic Gardens; *canadensis* refers to its wide range in Canada. Russet refers to the color of twigs and undersides of leaves. Also called soapberry, soopolallie and Canadian buffaloberry. Soapberry and soopolallie refer to the frothy lather fruits make when beaten.

Compare with: silver buffaloberry, mockorange, viburnums, boxwood.

Form: Erect deciduous shrub; 8–12 feet tall; rarely a small tree reaching 20 feet tall.

Leaves: Pinnately compound (9–13 leaflets), alternate, deciduous. Leaflets narrowly oblong to lanceolate; 1–3 inches long; margins sharply serrated for most of their length; tips pointed. Dark green and shiny above; paler green below.

Flowers/fruit: Tiny, white flowers borne in large, dense, flat-topped clusters (sometimes rounded) of 70–200. Fruits are small (¼- to ½-inch), round, orange to red pomes; no bloom.

Twigs/bark: Twigs stout with spur shoots. They are olive-drab when young and green-brown with age, with light-colored lenticels. Winter buds are sticky with white hairs. Bark is thin and gray-brown-green regardless of age.

Range/habitat: Ranges from Alaska to California and east into the Rockies, from sea level to subalpine. Typically grows on moist but well-drained soils on rocky hillsides, avalanche chutes, and forest clearings and near streams. Prefers open areas in forests and fields.

Notes: Hybridizes with *S. sitchensis*, creating specimens with intermediate characteristics. Indigenous people use infusions of its bark as a tonic, to relieve bed-wetting, and to reduce fever. Fruits and twigs are important food for many animals ranging from birds to bears; insects pollinate its flowers. Fruits are edible and used in wine. Wait to harvest until after several frosts to reduce bitterness.

Names: Rose family, *Rosaceae*. *Sorbus* is the Latin name for members of this genus; *scopulina* means of rocky places. Mountain-ash refers to its mountain habitat and ash-like compound leaves. Also called Greene, Cascade and western mountain-ash. Mountain-ash is hyphenated because it is not a true ash.

Compare with: other mountain-ashes, Oregon ash, elderberries.

Form: Erect deciduous shrub; 8–12 feet tall; shorter in rugged subalpine conditions; sometimes a small tree to 20 feet tall.

Leaves: Pinnately compound (seven to 11 leaflets), alternate, deciduous. Leaves 4–8 inches long; leaflets elliptical to oblong; 1–3 inches long; margins toothed above midpoint (highly variable); tips rounded. Green and smooth above; paler green below.

Flowers/fruit: Tiny, white flowers borne in large, dense, rounded clusters of 80 or fewer. Fruits are small (¼- to ½-inch), round, red pomes covered in bloom.

Twigs/bark: Twigs are stout with spur shoots. They are olive-drab when young; green-brown with age, with light-colored lenticels. Winter buds are rusty, not sticky. Bark is thin and gray-brown-green regardless of age.

Range/habitat: Ranges from Alaska to northern California and into western Montana in high-elevation coniferous forests and openings 2,500–10,000 feet. Grows on dry to moist sites in sun. Common along streams and above tree line.

Notes: Hybridizes with *S. scopulina*, creating specimens with intermediate characteristics. Common ornamental. Indigenous people use infusions of its roots and bark to relieve indigestion and rheumatism, rub berries in hair to control lice, and eat dried and boiled berries. Fruits and twigs are important food for many animals ranging from birds to bears. Used for streamside restoration. Reproduces mainly by seed but may also sprout from base.

Names: Rose family, *Rosaceae*. *Sorbus* is the Latin name for members of this genus; *sitchensis* refers to its presence around Sitka, Alaska. Mountain-ash refers to its mountain habitat and ash-like compound leaves. Also called western and Pacific mountain-ash. Mountain-ash is hyphenated because it is not a true ash.

Compare with: other mountain-ashes, Oregon ash, elderberries.

Form: Erect deciduous shrub; 2–6 feet tall. Commonly grows in moist thickets.

Leaves: Simple, alternate, deciduous. Oblong to elliptical; 1–3 inches long; margins toothed near apex but entire near base; petiole very short (less than ¼ inch). Green above; silvery pubescence below.

Flowers/fruit: Very small, pink to red flowers borne in dense, elongated (4–6 inches), upright clusters at branch ends. Fruits are small (about ⅛ inches), with brown follicles. They occur in upright, terminal clusters and persist through winter.

Twigs/bark: Twigs are slender, light yellow-brown when young; red-brown and slightly ribbed with age. Bark is red-brown and generally smooth but sometimes shreddy.

Range/habitat: Ranges from Alaska to northern California and east into Montana; sporadic pockets in a few eastern states. Grows primarily on wet sites such as stream banks, swales and near springs and seeps. Prefers full sun.

Notes: Indigenous people use its branches as brooms and to hang salmon and clams for preserving. Low browse value. Early successional species. Reproduces by seed, basal sprouts and rhizomes. Moderately fire resistant, perhaps because of its wet habitat; sprouts readily in response to damage.

Names: Rose family, *Rosaceae*. *Spiraea* is from Latin and means wreath (plants were often used to make bridal wreaths). *Douglasii* commemorates David Douglas, a Scottish botanist and plant explorer who spent several years in the Pacific Northwest. Also called rose or pink spirea, western spirea, hardhack and steeplebush.

Compare with: other spireas, serviceberry.

Form: Erect deciduous shrub usually less than 3 feet tall.

Leaves: Simple, alternate, deciduous. Elliptical, oval, ovate, or obovate; 1–1½ inches long; margins coarsely toothed near apex but entire near base; petiole very short (less than ¼ inch). Green and finely to sparsely hairy.

Flowers/fruit: Very small, pink to red flowers borne in dense, upright, pom-pom clusters at branch ends. Fruits are small (about ⅛-inch), brown follicles and occur in upright, terminal clusters. They persist through winter.

Twigs/bark: Twigs slender; tan when young; red-brown with age. Bark red-brown; often exfoliating on older twigs; smooth on larger, older stems.

Range/habitat: Grows from mid to high elevations in interior mountain ranges; 2,000–10,000 feet. Prefers open, wet sites such as stream banks, swales, springs and wet meadows but also occurs on rocky slopes.

Notes: Fragrant flowers attract butterflies. May hybridize with other spireas. Tea made from its stems, leaves and flowers is used to treat many ailments. Some Indigenous people use its flowers as paintbrushes for large paintings, such as those on tepees.

Names: Rose family, *Rosaceae*. *Spiraea* is from Latin and means wreath (plants were often used to make bridal wreaths). *Splendens* refers to its splendid flowers. Also called mountain, rosy, subalpine, Sierra and dense-flowered spirea. Also classified as *S. densiflora*.

Compare with: other spireas, serviceberry.

Form: Finely branched, upright deciduous shrub to 6 feet tall. Commonly forms dense thickets.

Leaves: Simple, opposite, deciduous. Shape highly variable; generally oval but may be elliptical to nearly round; ¾–2½ inches long. Margins vary from entire to shallowly lobed on the same plant and same stem. Green above; paler green below. Typically smooth above and slightly pubescent below (variable).

Flowers/fruit: Small (¼-inch), pink-white, bell-shaped flowers borne in small, terminal clusters; corolla densely hairy inside. Fruits are round, white, waxy berries, ¼–½ inch in diameter. Fruits often appear in clusters of three to five; the insides resemble snow crystals. Fruits last well into winter. They are commonly listed as toxic to humans and may cause nausea and vomiting.

Twigs/bark: Opposite branching. Twigs slender, smooth, yellow-brown. Pith orange-brown and hollow. Bark thin and tan to gray-brown. Bark often splits lengthwise on older stems.

Range/habitat: Widespread across North America; several eastern states consider it rare or endangered, but it's common over much of its range. Grows on a wide variety of sites; dry to moist; sun and shade.

Notes: Important browse for many species of wildlife and domestic animals. Important cover species for small animals. Birds and small mammals eat its berries. Spreads primarily by rhizomes and sprouts well after fire. Indigenous people use it as soap, to treat wounds and sores, and to soothe runny eyes. Common ornamental.

Names: Honeysuckle family, *Caprifoliaceae*. *Symphoricarpos* means fruit borne together; *albus* refers to its white fruit. The common name, snowberry, also refers to its white fruit. Also called common snowberry and white coralberry.

Compare with: creeping snowberry, black twinberry, mockorange.

Form: Trailing, deciduous shrub to 2 feet tall; branches may reach 3–6 feet long.

Leaves: Simple, opposite, deciduous. Shape highly variable; generally oval but may be elliptical to nearly round; ½–1 inch long; margins vary from entire to deeply lobed on the same plant and same stem. Green above; paler green below; usually pubescent on both surfaces.

Flowers/fruit: Small (¼-inch), pink-white, bell-shaped flowers borne in small, terminal clusters; corolla has only a few hairs inside. Fruits are round, white, waxy berries; ¼–½ inch in diameter. They are often clustered in groups of three to five. Fruits last well into winter. They are likely toxic to humans; may cause nausea and vomiting.

Twigs/bark: Opposite branching. Twigs slender and yellow-brown. Young twigs may be hairy. Pith hollow. Bark is thin and tan to gray-brown.

Range/habitat: Limited to the West Coast; much smaller range than common snowberry. Typically grows on dry, sunny, warm slopes from low to high elevations.

Notes: Indigenous people use its leaves to treat wounds and sores and use tea made from the bark to treat tuberculosis and venereal disease. May be toxic to mammals. Birds eat its fruits. Reproduces by rhizomes. Considered a weak sprouter after fire because shallow rhizomes are often killed. Seeds are not stored for long periods in the soil.

Names: Honeysuckle family, *Caprifoliaceae*. *Symphoricarpos* means fruit borne together; *mollis* means soft. Also called spreading snowberry and trailing snowberry. Creeping, trailing and spreading all refer to its growth form.

Compare with: common snowberry, black twinberry, mockorange.

Form: Erect shrub 3–10 feet tall or tree-climbing vine of almost limitless size.

Leaves: Pinnately compound (usually three leaflets but sometimes five), alternate, deciduous. Leaflets ovate to obovate. The terminal leaflet is usually larger than lateral leaflets. Lateral leaflets are irregularly lobed on one side and nearly entire on the other. In autumn, leaves turn brilliant red in sun or yellow in shade.

Flowers/fruit: Small, inconspicuous, yellow-green flowers borne in long-stemmed, hanging clusters. Fruits are small, round drupes that hang in elongated clusters. Their gray-white outer skin covers a white seed with black striations (pumpkin-like).

Twigs/bark: Twigs slender; light brown or tan; short, stiff lateral branchlets and tendrils. Buds naked; pubescent. Bark tan and smooth when young; gray-brown and rough with age.

Range/habitat: Occurs on moist to dry, well-drained sites in full sun or shade. Most common in valleys and foothills, often in pastures and along fencerows where birds deposit seeds.

Notes: All plant parts contain urushiol, an oil that causes a severe, itching rash (dermal toxicity) in most people year-round. Fumes of burning plants and touching animals that have walked through it trigger allergic reactions in many people. Many animals browse the plant with immunity. Bees make honey (to which people are not allergic) from the nectar. Interestingly, Lewis and Clark did not report seeing poisonoak.

Names: Cashew family, *Anacardiaceae*. *Toxicodendron* refers to its toxic nature; *diversilobum* refers to the diverse size, shape and number of lobes on leaves. Also called Pacific poisonoak. Poisonoak may be written as one word or hyphenated but is not written as separate words because it is not related to oaks. Formerly classified as *Rhus diversiloba*.

Compare with: poisonivy, wild blackberry, Oregon white oak.

Form: Erect shrub 2–10 feet tall. Unlike relatives Pacific poisonoak and eastern poisonivy, western poisonivy does not grow as a climbing vine; it has no aerial roots or tendrils.

Leaves: Compound (in sets of three), alternate and deciduous. Leaflets commonly 1-6 inches long and 1-4 inches wide. The terminal leaflet is the largest of the three and is usually symmetrically lobed; lobing on lateral leaflets is variable.

Flowers/fruit: Flowers quite small with five greenish-white petals in elongated clusters of fewer than 25 flowers. Fruits are small, dry drupes hanging in clusters, each with a single seed covered in a papery skin. Male and female flowers occur on separate plants (dioecious).

Twigs/bark: Thin-barked, sparsely branched and hairless, without aerial roots. Usually tan.

Range/habitat: Western poisonivy is native to much of North America. In the Northwest it grows primarily east of the Cascade crest, although it meanders westward through the Columbia Gorge to Cascade Locks. There, it mingles with Pacific poisonoak. East of the Cascades, it grows primarily along rivers and streams that wind throughout the high desert, so boaters beware. Even farther east, it climbs into dry, low elevation forests, on rocky slopes, and along roads. Eventually, it mingles and hybridizes with eastern poisonivy.

Notes: All parts of this plant contain urusiol, a chemical causing severe skin rashes in most humans during all times of the year. Both smoke and pet fur also transfer the chemical. Plants spread by seed and underground rhizomes, resulting in dense clumps. Native Americans reportedly used it in dyes and for medicine. Leaves turn yellow and orange in the fall.

Names: Cashew family, Anacardiaceae. Toxicodendron refers to its toxic nature. Poisonivy is not actually an ivy (*Hedera*) so its common name is most often hyphenated or joined together into one word, but it is also written as separate words. Unfortunately, there is no final arbiter in this decision. Formerly grouped in the genus *Rhus*.

Compare with: Pacific poisonoak, wild blackberry, eastern poisonivy.

Form: Dense, spiny evergreen shrub; prostrate to 10 feet tall. Grows in impenetrable thickets along the coast.

Leaves: Leaves trifoliate on young plants; mostly reduced to spines and scales on older plants; alternate; persistent. Spines 1–2 inches long; dark green; ribbed.

Flowers/fruit: Small (about 1 inch long), bright yellow, pealike flowers are profuse, often covering plants. Pollinating insects trigger explosive pollen release. Fruits are flattened pods; ½–1 inch long; green turning brown or black. Most seeds fall straight down; some pods twist open violently, expelling seeds up to 20 feet from the plant.

Twigs/bark: Twigs green to gray-green; ribbed; covered in dense spines. Green stems photosynthesize.

Range/habitat: Native to Europe, where it is an important component of coastal and heath communities. Introduced to North America in the 1800s as an ornamental and hedge plant. It soon escaped cultivation and is now common along both coasts. Extremely invasive; a noxious weed.

Notes: Fire-related species; volatile oils in spines and stems make it highly flammable. Fire opens seedpods and stimulates seed germination and sprouting. Gorse contributed to the burning of Bandon, Oregon, in 1936. Root nodules fix nitrogen, so it easily colonizes sand dunes, eroded lands and burned sites. Browsed by some animals; can be fed to domestic animals. Birds and ants help disperse its seeds. Ancient Celtic culture associated its bright yellow flowers with the sun.

Names: Legume family, *Fabaceae*. *Ulex* is the ancient Latin name for this plant; *europaeus* refers to its European heritage. Gorse may derive from an Anglo-Saxon word meaning wasteland. Other common names, at least in Europe, include furze, furse and whin.

Compare with: Scotch broom.

Form: Low-growing, highly branched deciduous shrub; erect but mat forming; usually less than 18 inches tall.

Leaves: Simple, alternate, deciduous. Elliptical to obovate or oblanceolate (widest above midpoint); small (½–2 inches long); margins toothed from apex to midpoint or below; apex acute to rounded; strong networked vein pattern below. Light green above; paler green below.

Flowers/fruit: Small (¼-inch long), white to red, narrowly urn-shaped flowers borne singly in leaf axils; twice as long as wide; flowers in late spring or summer after leaves emerge. Fruits are small (¼- to ½-inch), delicious blue berries covered in white bloom.

Twigs/bark: Young twigs are yellow-green; round to angled; glaucous and smooth to finely hairy. Bark is thin, smooth to shreddy and red-gray.

Range/habitat: Widely distributed across North America at high latitudes and elevations. Often occurs in openings in spruce-fir forests. Typically associated with bogs, swamps, open tundra and mosquitos.

Notes: Difficult to distinguish from *V. uliginosum* and *V. deliciosum* because all have great variation in leaves, flowers and fruit. Short stature seems to limit winter browse value since it is typically under snow. Its berries are important food for wildlife ranging from birds to bears to humans. Fire and scarification can damage its shallow roots and rhizomes, but resprouting typically occurs. Reproduces by seed (uncommon) and rhizomes.

Names: Heath family, *Ericaceae*. *Vaccinium* is the Latin name for this group of plants; *caespitosum* means tufted. Dwarf refers to its small stature, but it is not very different from other matted huckleberries, such as *V. uliginosum* and *V. deliciosum*. Also called dwarf blueberry, dwarf huckleberry and swamp bilberry.

Compare with: other small, deciduous huckleberry species.

Form: Low-growing deciduous shrub; matted to erect; usually less than 18 inches tall. Occurs in small clumps to dense colonies at high elevations.

Leaves: Simple, alternate, deciduous. Small (½–1½ inches); obovate to oblanceolate; thin; upper end toothed but not bottom; apex rounded; wedge-shaped base. Green above; paler green below, often with bloom.

Flowers/fruit: Small (¼-inch long), white to red, urn-shaped to nearly round flowers are borne in leaf axils; one to four per axil; usually four lobes. Delicious fruits are small (⅜–½-inch), blue berries covered in white bloom.

Twigs/bark: Twigs are yellow-green when young, turning red-gray with age. They are smooth or hairy, generally round and not angled. Bark is thin, smooth to shreddy and red-gray.

Range/habitat: Distributed across the Northern Hemisphere at high latitudes and elevations. Typically associated with bogs, swamps, open tundra, subalpine meadows and mosquitos.

Notes: Berries are an important traditional food for Indigenous people. They can be eaten raw or cooked in sauces. Many birds and mammals, ranging from bluebirds to grouse and mice to bears, eat its fruits. Its leaves are a favored browse of deer, elk, caribou and moose. Cascade bilberry eproduces effectively by seed, basal sprouts and rhizomes. It typically roots in the organic layer. Fire generally destroys seeds and shallow rhizomes, so recolonization can be slow.

Names: Heath family, *Ericaceae*. *Vaccinium* is the Latin name for this group of plants; *deliciosum* refers to the taste of its fruits. Also called Cascade blueberry; blue refers to its distinctively blue fruits.

Compare with: other small, deciduous huckleberry species.

Form: Erect or spreading deciduous shrub; 3–4 feet tall.

Leaves: Simple, alternate, deciduous. Small (½–2 inches long); elliptical, ovate or obovate. Margins are finely toothed. The apex is acute and the base is rounded. Pale green and slightly glaucous above; paler below. Leaves turn beautiful red to purple in fall.

Flowers/fruit: Small (¼-inch), solitary, nodding, pinkish flowers borne singly in leaf axils. The corolla is fused and urn-shaped to nearly round. Fruits are delicious small (¼- to ½-inch), purple to black berries almost without bloom.

Twigs/bark: Young branches are yellow-green to red and somewhat angled. Older branches and bark are gray and shreddy.

Range/habitat: Mountain species most common above 3,000 feet. The shrub has a wide ecological amplitude and is found in many conditions. Thinleaf huckleberry grows and flowers best in full sun but will also grow in dry or moist coniferous forests.

Notes: Fruits are among the most prized of all western huckleberries. The plant is deeply embedded in Northwest Indians' culture. Indigenous people eat its fruits raw and dried, use the fruits in a variety of medicines and have many rituals surrounding fruit picking and use. Berry production decreases with increasing forest cover and fire control. The shrub reproduces best after wildfire, when it sprouts from the root collar and extensive rhizome system. It is pollinated by bees, and its berries are a key food for black and grizzly bears. It is of variable browse value.

Names: Heath family, *Ericaceae*. *Vaccinium* is the Latin name for this group of plants; *membranaceum* means skinlike and may refer to its thin leaves or translucent flowers. Also called big, mountain and black huckleberry and big whortleberry.

Compare with: other huckleberries, false huckleberry, native azaleas.

Form: Small, upright deciduous shrub; commonly 4–18 inches tall.

Leaves: Simple, alternate, deciduous. Small (½–1½ inches long); ovate to lanceolate; margins finely toothed; apex acute to obtuse; strongly veined on lower surface. Green above, paler green below, and red, yellow or brown in fall.

Flowers/fruit: Small (¼-inch long), green-white to pink, bell-shaped to nearly round, waxy flowers borne singly in leaf axils. Fruits are small (¼-inch), purple to dark red berries with no bloom.

Twigs/bark: Young twigs are green and strongly angled. Short hairs appear in grooves, and they may become red in sun. Buds are typically light green. Mature bark is typically red-gray.

Range/habitat: Grows around the world at high latitudes and elevations. In the Pacific Northwest, whortleberry grows in mid- to high-elevation coniferous forests from British Columbia south to Central Oregon east of the Cascades. It also grows in southwest Oregon and throughout the Rockies, where it's most common.

Notes: Reproduces by seed, basal sprouts and rhizomes. Birds and mammals disperse its seeds widely. It commonly sprouts from rhizomes after disturbance and appears well-adapted to frequent, light fires. Browse value is high for small mammals but low for larger animals. Many birds, small mammals and bears favor its fruits. Though small, the berries are edible and important for some Indigenous people. Many medicinal properties are attributed to this plant and its close relatives.

Names: Heath family, *Ericaceae*. *Vaccinium* is the Latin name for this group of plants; *myrtillus* means similar to a small myrtle. Also called dwarf bilberry, dwarf blueberry, and myrtle blueberry.

Compare with: other small, deciduous huckleberry species.

Form: Erect, slender, spreading shrub; 1–12 feet tall; often kept short and bushy by browsing.

Leaves: Simple, alternate, deciduous. 1–1½ inches long; oval and rounded at both ends; margins typically entire but sometimes inconspicuously toothed. Green above; paler green below.

Flowers/fruit: Small (about ¼-inch long), pinkish, globular, tubular to urn-shaped flowers borne singly in leaf axils. "Bells" are usually longer than wide and usually appear before, or sometimes with, leaves. Fruits are small (¼- to ½-inch), blue-black berries with a blue-white bloom. They are tart but flavorful.

Twigs/bark: Young twigs are typically yellow-green but may turn red in sun. They're slender, conspicuously angled and grooved with strong ribs. They appear almost winged. Older branches are gray. Bark is rosy when new and gray and exfoliating with age.

Range/habitat: Grows at mid to subalpine elevations, but also at low elevations, in the northern half of the Pacific Northwest. Disjunct populations occur in central and eastern North America. They're common in gaps and openings in moist coniferous forests and near boggy areas.

Notes: One of the most commonly collected berries. Oval-leaf huckleberry is highly regarded by Indigenous people. It ripens earlier than other huckleberries and is high in nutrients and energy content. Fruits are an important food for grizzly bears and other wildlife. The shrubs are browsed by many species, but palatability varies by site and season. It reproduces by seed but especially by basal sprouts, layering and rhizomes. Hybridizes with related species.

Names: Heath family, *Ericaceae. Vaccinium* is the Latin name for this group of plants; *ovalifolium* refers to its oval-shaped leaves. Also called oval-leaf blueberry. Some taxonomists now consider *V. alaskaense* and *V. ovalifolium* a single species.

Compare with: other deciduous huckleberry species.

Form: Stiff, upright, broadleaved evergreen shrub; commonly 2–15 feet tall.

Leaves: Simple, alternate, persistent; distinctly two-ranked. Small (½–1½ inches long); ovate; margins finely serrated. Thick and leathery; dark green and waxy above; paler green below.

Flowers/fruit: Small (¼-inch long), white to pink, bell-shaped flowers borne in small clusters in leaf axils; often fragrant. Fruits are small (¼-inch), tasty blue-black berries. They occur in tight clusters close to twigs and last long into winter.

Twigs/bark: Twigs slender and red-brown. They are pubescent when young and smooth with age. Young twigs are often ridged. Buds have bright red, imbricate scales. Bark is thin, smooth and red-brown. Bark is often difficult to see because of the shrub's dense foliage.

Range/habitat: Evergreen huckleberry ranges from British Columbia through California. It is more common in the Coast Range than in the Cascades. It grows on moist, well-drained, sandy and gravelly sites in sun or shade. This shrub is very tolerant of shade and understory conditions.

Notes: Foliage is an important cash crop, commonly used by florists. Evergreen huckleberry is a common ornamental. Indigenous people eat its fruits raw, cooked, mashed into cakes and in jam and sauces. Deer and elk browse its foliage, but value seems variable. Many animals eat its fruits, and dense thickets create cover for smaller animals. The shrub reproduces by copious seeds and basal sprouting.

Names: Heath family, *Ericaceae*. *Vaccinium* is the Latin name for this group of plants; *ovatum* refers to its ovate leaves. Also called California huckleberry and box huckleberry.

Compare with: other huckleberries, Oregon boxwood.

Form: Upright, finely branched deciduous shrub, commonly 4–12 feet tall.

Leaves: Simple, alternate, deciduous. Leaves on mature plants are small (½–1½ inches long) and elliptical to ovate. Margins entire; very thin. Green above; paler green below. Leaves on juvenile plants are very small and finely serrated. The leaves commonly persist through winter.

Flowers/fruit: Small (¼-inch long), green-white or pink, bell-shaped to flattened, round flowers borne singly in leaf axils. Fruits are small (¼-inch), bright red berries with translucent skin. Berries are tart but delicious.

Twigs/bark: Young twigs bright green and ribbed or angled. Buds are small and red; they contrast starkly with twigs. Bark is thin, smooth and red-brown.

Range/habitat: Grows on a wide variety of sites in full sun to full shade from southeast Alaska to central California; 0–5,000 feet. Often grows on rotting logs and stumps. Moisture in logs helps it survive summer droughts, and increased height helps protect it from browsing.

Notes: Its berries are highly regarded by wildlife and humans and are an important traditional food for Indigenous people, but berry production is not typically heavy. Many birds and mammals, ranging from bluebirds to grouse and mice to bears, eat its fruits. The leaves are favored browse of deer, elk and mountain goats, which often nip plants to the ground. Reproduces effectively by seed, basal sprouts and rhizomes.

Names: Heath family, *Ericaceae*. *Vaccinium* is the Latin name for this group of plants; *parvifolium* refers to its small leaves. Red refers to bright red berries, which are uncommon among huckleberries.

Compare with: other deciduous huckleberry species.

Form: Low-growing, highly branched deciduous shrub; usually erect but sometimes matted; usually less than 18 inches tall.

Leaves: Simple, alternate, deciduous. Small (½-inch long); elliptical to ovate; margins finely serrated but appear entire from a distance. Green above; paler green and glabrous below.

Flowers/fruit: Small (¼-inch long), pink, urn-shaped, inconspicuous flowers borne singly. Fruits are small (¼-inch), red berries. They're edible but tiny.

Twigs/bark: Twigs green when young and red-gray with age. Angled, resembling a whisk broom. Bark is thin, more or less smooth and red-gray.

Range/habitat: Grows in subalpine forests from British Columbia to California, mostly on the east side, and east throughout the Rockies. Sites are often characterized by heavy snowpack, summer drought and short growing seasons.

Notes: Berries are highly regarded by wildlife and humans but difficult to pick. Its berries are a common traditional food for Indigenous people, and its branches are used as brooms. Leaves are eaten by many animals but not highly palatable. Fruits are eaten by a wide array of birds and mammals and favored by grouse and ptarmigans. Shallow rhizomes make plants susceptible to fire damage and human-caused soil disturbances, such as logging and site preparation. Reproduces by seed and rhizomes. Because seedlings are fragile, rhizomes may be most important.

Names: Heath family, *Ericaceae*. *Vaccinium* is the Latin name for this group of plants; *scoparium* means "like a broom" and refers to its broom-like branches. The common name refers to preference by grouse. Also called grouse huckleberry, grouseberry and littleleaf huckleberry.

Compare with: other small, deciduous huckleberry species.

Form: Low-growing, highly branched deciduous shrub; matted to erect; usually less than 18 inches tall.

Leaves: Simple, alternate, deciduous. Small (½–1 inches long); elliptical to obovate; margins entire; apex rounded but with a slight tip; strong networked vein pattern below. Firm to leathery; often distinctly blue above but may be green; paler green below.

Flowers/fruit: Small (¼-inch long), pink, narrowly urn-shaped flowers borne in leaf axils; one to four per axil; usually four lobes. Fruits are small (¼– to ½-inch), delicious blue berries covered in white bloom.

Twigs/bark: Twigs yellow-green when young, red-gray with age. They're hairy, round and not angled. Bark is thin, smooth to shreddy, red-gray.

Range/habitat: Distributed across the Northern Hemisphere at high latitudes and elevations. Typically associated with bogs, swamps, open tundra and mosquitos.

Notes: Berries are highly regarded by wildlife and humans and an important traditional food for Indigenous people. Many birds and mammals, ranging from bluebirds to grouse and mice to bears, eat its fruits. The leaves are favored browse of deer, elk, caribou and moose. Reproduces effectively by seed, basal sprouts and rhizomes. It typically roots in the organic layer. Fire generally destroys seeds and shallow rhizomes, so recolonization can be slow.

Names: Heath family, *Ericaceae*. *Vaccinium* is the Latin name for this group of plants; *uliginosum* refers to growing in bogs or swamps. Blue refers to its distinctively blue fruits. Also called dwarf and alpine blueberry; huckleberry, bilberry and whortleberry are often substituted for the word blueberry.

Compare with: other small, deciduous huckleberry species.

Form: Mat-forming, creeping evergreen shrub; usually less than 1 foot tall. Slender stems root adventitiously, helping create this form.

Leaves: Simple, alternate and persistent. Small (½–1 inch long); obovate to elliptical. Margins appear entire from a distance but are minutely toothed and slightly revolute. The apex is often slightly notched and the petiole short. Thick; green and shiny above; light green below. The underside is dotted with sparse, short, stiff hairs that are light colored when young but turn black with age. They may turn purple in autumn.

Flowers/fruit: One to several small (about ¼ inch long), white to pink, nodding, bell-shaped flowers borne on short stalks at twig ends. Fruits are small (¼- to ½-inch), bright red berries; edible but sour.

Twigs/bark: Twigs slender and trailing, light brown to yellow. They root at nodes. Branches minutely pubescent. Bark hard to see because plants hug the ground.

Range/habitat: Common in spruce and birch forests of the boreal regions of North America, Eurasia and Japan. Forms loose mats in moist, mossy conditions and dense mats on dry, rocky slopes in arctic and alpine areas. Tolerates cold, harsh sites.

Notes: Its berries have a sweeter flavor than cranberries. They're very good for jam, jelly and relish. Berries are readily eaten by ptarmigans, grouse, bears, caribou, reindeer and other animals. Indigenous people use its fruits and leaves for food and medicines. Seedlings are rare in the field; it reproduces mostly by rhizomes.

Names: Heath family, *Ericaceae*. *Vaccinium* is the Latin name for this group of plants; *vitis-idaea* refers to "vine of Mount Ida," a sacred mountain in Greek mythology. Lingonberry is derived from a similar Scandinavian name. Also called mountain cranberry and lowbush cranberry.

Compare with: bog cranberry, kinnikinnick, evergreen huckleberry, mahala mat.

Form: Loosely branched deciduous shrub with several to many stems; 3–12 feet tall.

Leaves: Simple, opposite, deciduous. Round, oval, or obovate; palmately lobed and toothed (typically three lobes), but some are unlobed. Leaves are 2–5 inches long with the petiole about 1 inch. Green and glabrous above; paler and finely pubescent below.

Flowers/fruit: Small (about ¼-inch), white flowers borne in terminal clusters about 1 inch wide. Fruits are ellipsoidal (¼–½ inch long), orange to red drupes (like cherries) with a single, flattened seed. They're edible but tart.

Twigs/bark: Twigs opposite and slender, green turning red-brown and eventually gray. Bark smooth and gray.

Range/habitat: Grows across Canada and Alaska south through many northern states. Highbush cranberry migrates south along the Rockies to Colorado. Occurs in coniferous and deciduous forests; it's most common on moist sites. Develops best in full sun but tolerates shade; may dominate the understory on some sites.

Notes: Many mammals and birds, especially bears, eat its fruits. Beavers, rabbits, hares and moose eat its leaves, which have moderate browse value. Common ornamental. Makes excellent jam and jelly; traditionally used to treat colds and sore throats. Seeds are stored in the soil; disturbance aids germination. Plants root and produce rhizomes in organic matter. They sprout easily from base roots.

Names: Honeysuckle family, *Caprifoliaceae*. *Viburnum* is the Latin name for this group of plants; *edule* means edible. Its tart fruits remind some of cranberries, but they are not related. Also called squashberry, lowbush cranberry (although much taller than true cranberries), mooseberry and moosewood viburnum.

Compare with: western wayfaring tree.

Form: Erect, loosely branched deciduous shrub or small tree; 3–12 feet tall.

Leaves: Simple, opposite, deciduous. Elliptical to almost round; 1–3 inches long; coarsely and bluntly toothed, especially near apex. Venation is arcuate with three to five conspicuous veins from base. Petioles are covered in spreading, coarse hairs and often short, raised glands. Dark green and glabrous above; lighter green below with short, stiff hairs. Foliage is brilliant red in fall.

Flowers/fruit: Small (about ¼- to ⅓-inch), white flowers borne in rounded or flat-topped, terminal clusters about 1–2 inches wide; stamens are longer than petals. Fruits are ellipsoidal (½ inch long), purple to black drupes (like cherries) with a large, flattened, stonelike, grooved seed.

Twigs/bark: Twigs opposite; slender; keeled and ribbed below leaf scars; gray with shades of green or red. Lenticels inconspicuous on young twigs; warty with age. Bud scales are red-brown; hairy along margins. Bark gray-red-brown.

Range/habitat: Grows from southern Washington to California west of the Cascades and Sierras. Common along edges of deciduous woods and near streams with winter flooding and summer drought. Prefers open woods and thickets.

Notes: Some *Viburnum* fruits are edible, but some are not. Don't take chances. Some Indigenous people make necklaces from its fruits. Its flowers are attractive to birds and butterflies.

Names: Honeysuckle family, *Caprifoliaceae*. *Viburnum* is the Latin name for this group of plants; *ellipticum* refers to its elliptical leaves, though they're not as elliptical as those of many other shrubs. Wayfaring tree is a common name for many *Viburnum* species. Also called western, common and oval-leafed viburnum.

Compare with: highbush cranberry.

Publications

Gilkey, H.M., and L.J. Dennis. 2001. Handbook of Northwestern Plants (Rev. ed.) Corvallis, OR: Oregon State University Press.

Hitchcock, C.L., and A. Cronquist. (© 1973) 1976. Flora of the Pacific Northwest. Third printing with further corrections. Seattle, WA: University of Washington Press.

Jensen, E.C., W.R. Randall, R.F. Keniston and D.N. Bever. 2012. Manual of Oregon Trees and Shrubs (10th ed.). Corvallis, OR: John Bell and Associates.

Jensen, E.C. 2021. Trees to Know in Oregon. EC 1450. Corvallis, OR: Oregon State University Extension Service.

Johnson, D., L. Kerhaw, A. MacKinnon and J. Pojar. 1995. Plants of the Western Boreal Forest and Aspen Parkland. Edmonton, Alberta, Canada: Lone Pine Publishing.

Lyons, C.P. 1999. Trees and Shrubs of Washington. Edmonton, Alberta, Canada: Lone Pine Publishing.

Parish, R., R. Coupe and D. Lloyd. 1999. Plants of Southern Interior British Columbia and the Inland Northwest (2nd ed.). Edmonton, Alberta, Canada: Lone Pine Publishing.

Pojar, J., and A. MacKinnon. 2004. Plants of the Pacific Northwest Coast (Rev. ed.). Edmonton, Alberta, Canada: Lone Pine Publishing.

Viereck, L.A., and E.L. Little Jr. 2007. Alaska Trees and Shrubs (2nd ed.). Fairbanks, AK: University of Alaska Press.

Websites

Botanary, the Botanical Dictionary. Dave's Garden. http://davesgarden.com/guides/botanary/

Burke Museum of Natural History and Culture. University of Washington. http://www.burkemuseum.org/

CalPhotos [photo database]. Biodiversity Sciences Technology Group, Berkeley Natural History Museums, University of California, Berkeley. http://calphotos.berkeley.edu/

Canada's Plant Hardiness Site. Canadian Forest Service. http://planthardiness.gc.ca/

Dendrology at Virginia Tech. Department of Forest Resources and Environmental Conservation, Virginia Polytechnic Institute and State University. https://dendro.cnre.vt.edu/dendrology/main.htm

E-FLORA BC: Electronic Atlas of the Flora of British Columbia. Department of Geography, University of British Columbia. http://eflora.bc.ca

Fire Effects Information System. USDA Forest Service. https://www.feis-crs.org/feis/

Integrated Taxonomic Information System. http://www.itis.gov

The Jepson Flora Project. The Jepson Herbarium, University of California, Berkeley. Main site: http://ucjeps.berkeley.edu/jepson_flora_project.html

Lady Bird Johnson Wildflower Center. The University of Texas at Austin. http://wildflower.org/

Landscape Plants: Images, Identification, and Information. Department of Horticulture, Oregon State University. http://oregonstate.edu/dept/ldplants/

Native American Ethnobotany. University of Michigan, Dearborn. http://naeb.brit.org

Oregon Flora Project. Department of Botany and Plant Pathology, Oregon State University. http://oregonflora.org/

Seiler, J. R., J. Peterson and E.C. Jensen. 2105, 4th ed. Woody Plants in North America. Kendall Hunt Publishing Company. he.kendallhunt.company/product/woody-plants-north-america.

USDA PLANTS Database. USDA Natural Resources Conservation Service. http://plants.usda.gov

Use the checkboxes to keep track of which species you find on your adventures in Pacific Northwest forests. (Note: Checkboxes are not included for alternate scientific names or synonyms.)

Acer, 34–35
- ☐ *circinatum*, 34
- ☐ *glabrum*, 35
- ☐ *glabrum* var. *douglasii*, 35

Alnus, 36–37
- ☐ *incana*, 36
- ☐ *incana* ssp. *tenuifolia*, 36
- ☐ *viridis*, 37
- ☐ *viridis* ssp. *sinuata*, 37

☐ *Amelanchier alnifolia*, 38

Arctostaphylos, 39–42
- ☐ *columbiana*, 39
- ☐ *patula*, 40
- ☐ *uva-ursi*, 41
- ☐ *viscida*, 42

☐ *Artemisia tridentata*, 43

☐ *Baccharis pilularis*, 44

Berberis, 45–47
- ☐ *aquifolium*, 45
- ☐ *nervosa*, 46
- ☐ *repens*, 47

☐ *Betula glandulosa*, 48

Ceanothus, 49–55
- ☐ *cordulatus*, 49
- ☐ *cuneatus*, 50
- ☐ *integerrimus*, 51
- ☐ *prostratus*, 52
- ☐ *sanguineus*, 53
- ☐ *thrysiflorus*, 54
- ☐ *velutinus*, 55

☐ *Celtis reticulata*, 56

Cercocarpus, 57–58
- ☐ *betuloides*, 57
- ☐ *ledifolius*, 58
- *montanus*, 57

☐ *Chrysolepis sempervirens,* 59

☐ *Chrysothamnus nauseosus,* 67

☐ *Clematis ligusticifolia*, 60

Cornus, 61
- ☐ *sericea*, 61
- ☐ *sericea* var. *occidentalis*, 61
- *stolonifera,* 61

Corylus, 62
- ☐ *cornuta*, 62
- ☐ *cornuta* var. *californica*, 62

Crataegus, 63–64
- *columbiana*, 63
- ☐ *douglasii*, 63
- ☐ *monogyna*, 64

☐ *Cytisus scoparius*, 65

☐ *Dasiphora fruticosa*, 66

☐ *Ericameria nauseosa*, 67

Frangula (Rhamnus), 89–90

Garrya, 68–69
- ☐ *elliptica*, 68
- ☐ *fremontii*, 69

☐ *Gaultheria shallon*, 70

☐ *Holodiscus discolor*, 71

☐ *Juniperus communis*, 72

Lonicera, 73–76
- ☐ *ciliosa*, 73
- ☐ *conjugialis*, 74
- ☐ *hispidula*, 75
- ☐ *involucrata*, 76

Mahonia (Berberis), 45–47

☐ *Malus fusca*, 77

☐ *Menziesia ferruginea*, 78

Morella (Myrica), 79

☐ *Myrica californica*, 79

☐ *Oemleria cerasiformis*, 80

☐ *Oplopanax horridus (horridum)*, 81

☐ *Paxistima myrsinites*, 82

☐ *Philadelphus lewisii*, 83

☐ *Physocarpus capitatus*, 84

Potentilla (Dasiphora), 66

Prunus, 85–87
- ☐ *emarginata*, 85
- ☐ *subcordata*, 86
- ☐ *virginiana*, 87

☐ *Purshia tridentata*, 88

Rhamnus, 89–90
- ☐ *californica*, 89
- ☐ *purshiana*, 90

Rhododendron, 91–93
- ☐ *albiflorum*, 91
- ☐ *macrophyllum*, 92
- ☐ *occidentale*, 93

Rhus diversiloba, 121

Ribes, 94–101
- ☐ *aureum*, 94
- ☐ *bracteosum*, 95
- ☐ *cereum*, 96
- ☐ *divaricatum*, 97
- ☐ *lacustre*, 98
- ☐ *roezlii*, 99
- ☐ *sanguineum*, 100
- ☐ *viscosissimum*, 101

☐ *Rosa*, 102–103
- ☐ *canina*, 103
- ☐ *eglanteria*, 103
- ☐ *gymnocarpa*, 103
- ☐ *multiflora*, 103
- ☐ *nutkana*, 103
- ☐ *pisocarpa*, 103
- ☐ *woodsii*, 103

Rubus, 104–109
- *armeniacus,* 104
- *bifrons*, 104
- ☐ *discolor*, 104
- ☐ *laciniatus*, 105
- ☐ *leucodermins*, 106
- ☐ *parviflorus*, 107
- ☐ *spectabilis*, 108
- *ulmifolius*, 104
- ☐ *ursinus*, 109

☐ *Salix,* 110–111
- ☐ *bebbiana*, 111
- ☐ *geyeriana*, 111
- ☐ *hookeriana*, 111
- ☐ *lasiandra*, 111
- ☐ *lemmonii*, 111
- ☐ *prolixa*, 111
- ☐ *scouleriana*, 111
- ☐ *stichensis*, 111

Sambucus, 112–113
- ☐ *nigra*, 112
- ☐ *nigra* ssp. *cerulea*, 112
- ☐ *racemosa*, 113

☐ *Shepherdia canadensis*, 114

Sorbus, 115–116
- ☐ *scopulina*, 115
- ☐ *sitchensis*, 116

Spiraea, 117–118
- *densiflora*, 118
- ☐ *douglasii*, 117
- ☐ *splendens*, 118

Symphoricarpos, 119–120
- ☐ *albus*, 119
- ☐ *mollis*, 120

Toxicodendron
- ☐ *diversilobum, 121*
- ☐ *rydbergii, 122*

☐ *Ulex europaeus*, 123

Vaccinium, 124–133
- *alaskaense,* 128
- ☐ *caespitosum*, 124
- ☐ *deliciosum*, 125
- ☐ *membranaceum*, 126
- ☐ *myrtillus*, 127
- ☐ *ovalifolium*, 128
- ☐ *ovatum*, 129
- ☐ *parvifolium*, 130
- ☐ *scoparium*, 131
- ☐ *uglinosum*, 132
- ☐ *vitis-idaea*, 133

Viburnum, 134–135
- ☐ *edule*, 134
- ☐ *ellipticum*, 135

Use the checkboxes to keep track of which species you find on your adventures. (Note: Checkboxes are provided for the most common names.)

alder
- green, 37
- Sitka, 37
- speckled, 36
- thinleaf, 36

- antelope bush, 88
- apple (crabapple), 77

arrow-wood, 71

azalea
- Cascade, 91
- false, 78
- western, 93
  see also rhododendron

barberry
- Cascade, 46
- creeping western, 47

bayberry
- California, 79
- Pacific, 79

bearberry, 41, 76, 90

bear brush, 69

bilberry
- Cascade, 125
- dwarf, 124, 127
- swamp, 124
  see also blueberry, huckleberry, lingonberry, whortleberry

birch
- bog, 48
- dwarf, 48
- resin, 48
- scrub, 48
- shrub, 48
- swamp, 48

- bitterbrush, 88
- antelope, 88

blackberry
- California, 109
- cutleaf, 105
- evergreen, 105
- Himalayan (Himalaya), 104
- trailing, 109
- wild, 109
  see also raspberry, salmonberry, thimbleberry

blackcap, 106

blueberry
- alpine, 132
- bog, 132
- Cascade, 125
- dwarf, 124, 127, 132
- myrtle, 127
- oval-leaf, 128
  see also bilberry, huckleberry, lingonberry, whortleberry

blueblossom, 54

blue-brush, 54

blue-myrtle, 54

boxleaf, 82

boxwood
- mountain, 82
- Oregon, 82

- broom, Scotch (Scotchbroom), 65

buckbrush, 50, 53
- common, 50
- narrowleaf, 50
  see also ceanothus, deerbrush, mahala mat, snowbrush

buckthorn
- California, 89
- cascara, 90

buffaloberry
- Canadian, 114
- russet, 114

California-lilac, 54

ceanothus
- blueblossom, 54
- deerbrush, 51
- prostrate, 52
- redstem, 53
- snowbrush, 55
- varnish-leaf, 55
- wedgeleaf, 50
- whitethorn, 49
  see also buckbrush, deerbrush, mahala mat, snowbrush

cercocarpus
- birchleaf, 57
- curlleaf, 58

chamisa, 67

chaparral broom, 44

cherry
- bird, 80
- bitter, 85
  see also chokecherry, plum

chinquapin (chinkapin)
- bush, 59

chittam (chittim), 90

- chokecherry, 87
  see also cherry, plum

cinquefoil
- bush, 66
- shrubby, 66

clematis
- western white, 60
- white, 60

coffeeberry
- California, 89
- Sierra, 89

coffee-tree, 90

coralberry
- white, 119

- coyotebrush, 44

coyote bush, 44

crabapple (crab apple)
- Oregon, 77
- Pacific, 77
- western, 77

cranberry
- highbush, 134
- lowbush, 133, 134
- mountain, 133

creambush, 71

currant
- bristly black, 98
- buffalo, 94
- fragrant golden, 94
- golden, 94
- prickly, 98
- red-flowering, 100
- squaw, 96
- sticky, 101
- sticky flowering, 101
- stink, 95
- stinking, 95
- stinking black, 95
- swamp, 98
- wax, 96
  see also gooseberry

deerbrush, 51
  see also buckbrush, ceanothus, mahala mat, snowbrush

- devilsclub (devil's club), 81

devilwood, 34

dewberry
- western, 109

dogwood
- creek, 61
- red-osier, 61
- western, 61

elderberry (elder)
- black, 112
- blue, 112
- coast red, 113
- red, 113
- redberry, 113

English broom, 65

falsebox, 82

flannel bush, 69

furse (furze), 123

goldenbush, 67

gooseberry
- black, 97, 98
- black swamp, 98
- coastal black, 97
- shiny-leaved, 99
- Sierra, 99
- spreading, 97
- straggly, 97
  see also currant

- gorse, 123

greasewood, 50

grouseberry, 131

hackberry
- netleaf, 56
- western, 56

hardhack, 117

hawthorn
- black, 63
- Columbia, 63
- common, 64
- Douglas, 63
- English, 64
- oneseed, 64
- river, 63

hazel
- beaked, 62
- California, 62

Himalaya berry, 104

holly
- mountain, 47
- holly-grape (hollygrape), 47
- creeping, 46, 47
- hollyleaved barberry, 45

honeysuckle
- California, 76
- double, 74
- four-line, 76
- hairy, 75
- orange, 73
- pink, 75
- purpleflower, 74
- western trumpet, 73
  see also twinberry

huckleberry
  big, 126
  black, 126
  box, 129
  California, 129
  dwarf, 124
  ☐ evergreen, 129
  fool's, 78
  grouse, 131
  littleleaf, 131
  mountain, 126
  ☐ oval-leaf, 128
  ☐ red, 130
  ☐ thinleaf, 126
  see also bilberry,
    blueberry,
    lingonberry,
    whortleberry
☐ Indian-plum, 80
ironwood, 71
juneberry, 38
juniper
  ☐ common, 72
  dwarf, 72
  ground, 72
  prostrate, 72
kidneywort baccharis, 44
☐ kinnikinnick, 41
  see also manzanita
☐ lingonberry, 133
  see also blueberry,
    bilberry, huckleberry,
    whortleberry
☐ mahala mat, 52
  see also buckbrush,
    ceanothus,
    deerbrush,
    snowbrush
mahonia
  creeping, 46, 47
manzanita
  green, 40
  ☐ greenleaf, 40
  ☐ hairy, 39
  sticky, 42
  ☐ whiteleaf, 42
  see also kinnikinnick
maple
  ☐ Douglas, 35
  ☐ Rocky Mountain, 35
  ☐ vine, 34
mealberry, 41
☐ meadowsweet, rose, 118
  see also spirea
menziesia
  ☐ rusty, 78

☐ mockorange (mock-
    orange), 83
  Lewis', 83
mooseberry, 134
mountain-ash
  Cascade, 115
  ☐ Greene's (Greene), 115
  Pacific, 116
  ☐ Sitka, 116
  western, 115, 116
mountain lover, 82
mountain-mahogany
  ☐ birchleaf, 57
  ☐ curlleaf, 58
  desert, 58
  true, 57
mountain misery, 91
myrtle
  boxleaf, 82
☐ ninebark, 84
  Pacific, 84
☐ oceanspray, 71
octopus-of-the-woods, 34
old man's beard, 60
Oregon-grape
  Cascade, 46
  ☐ creeping, 47
  dull, 46
  ☐ dwarf, 46
  ☐ tall, 45
oso berry, 80
palo blanco, 56
pepper vine, 60
plum
  ☐ Klamath, 86
  Oregon, 86
  Sierra, 86
  see also cherry,
    chokecherry
poisonivy
  ☐ western, 122
☐ poisonoak (poison-
    oak), 121
  Pacific, 121
quinine bush, 69
rabbitbrush
  gray (grey), 67
  ☐ rubber, 67
raspberry
  ☐ black, 106
  western, 106
  western black, 106
  whitebark, 106
  see also blackberry,
    salmonberry,

rhododendron
  California, 92
  coast, 92
  ☐ Pacific, 92
  white, 91
  white-flowered, 91
  see also azalea
rose, 102–103
  ☐ clustered, 103
  ☐ dog, 103
  ☐ little wood, 103
  ☐ multiflora, 103
  ☐ Nootka, 103
  ☐ sweetbriar, 103
  ☐ Wood's, 103
rosebay
  California, 92
sagebrush
  basin big, 43
  ☐ big, 43
  mountain big, 43
  Wyoming big, 43
☐ salal, 70
☐ salmonberry, 108
  see also blackberry,
    raspberry,
    thimbleberry
serviceberry
  ☐ Pacific, 38
  Saskatoon, 38
  western, 38
shadbush
  western, 39
silktassel
  coast, 68
  ☐ Fremont's, 69
  ☐ wavyleaf, 68
skunk bush, 80
☐ snowberry, 119
  common, 119
  ☐ creeping, 120
  spreading, 120
  trailing, 120
☐ snowbrush, 55
  see also buckbrush,
    ceanothus,
    deerbrush,
    mahala mat
snow bush, 49
soapberry, 114
soapbloom, 53
soopolallie, 114

spirea
  dense-flowered, 118
  ☐ Douglas, 117
  mountain, 118
  pink, 117
  rose, 117
  rosy, 118
  Sierra, 118
  subalpine, 118
  western, 117
  see also
    meadowsweet, rose
squashberry, 134
squawcarpet, 52
steeplebush, 117
syringa, 83
☐ thimbleberry, 107
  western, 107
  see also blackberry,
    raspberry,
    salmonberry
tobacco bush, 55
traveller's joy, 60
twinberry, 76
  ☐ black, 76
  mountain, 74
  see also honeysuckle
viburnum
  common, 135
  moosewood, 134
  oval-leafed, 135
  western, 135
  see also cranberry,
    wayfaring tree
virgin's bower, 60
wayfaring tree
  ☐ western, 135
☐ waxmyrtle, 79
whin, 123
whitethorn
  mountain, 49
☐ whortleberry, 127
  big, 126
  ☐ grouse, 131
  see also blueberry,
    bilberry, huckleberry
willow, 110–111
  ☐ Bebb's, 111
  ☐ Geyer's, 111
  ☐ Hooker's, 111
  ☐ Lemmon's, 111
  ☐ McKenzie, 111
  ☐ Pacific, 111
  ☐ Scouler's, 111
  ☐ Sitka, 111

An endeavor like this book requires the support of many. At the risk of leaving someone out, I'd particularly like to thank the following people.

For influencing the content of the book:

- Friend and colleague David Zahler helped in ways too numerous to mention, especially with photo selection and development of range maps.

- Thousands of students in hundreds of classes helped me hone my own ability to identify and describe trees and shrubs, and students in recent classes helped refine the identification key and species descriptions in this book. Several deserve special mention for their efforts: Andrew Merschel, Chili Hunt, Carrie Black, Mary Grant and Sara Lynch. Gary Breed helped develop the range maps.

- Folks associated with the Oregon Flora Project, including Aaron Liston, Richard Halse and Linda Hardison, helped me understand the ever-changing world of taxonomy and nomenclature.

- Colleagues from Oregon State University's Forestry and Natural Resources Extension Program helped determine which species to include, helped me locate several rare species and continually urged me to press on.

- Folks at Seven Oaks Nursery in Corvallis, Oregon, made their native plant collection and expertise available on numerous occasions.

For improving the written and graphic elements of the book:

- Current and former colleagues from Oregon State University Extension Communications, especially Janet Donnelly, Alan Dennis, Jennifer Alexander, Mark Anderson-Wilk, Erik Simmons and Zak Eidsvoog.

For moral support and tolerance shown to a lover of forests:

- Family members Linda, Chris, Nick and Courtney endured an infinite number of unscheduled stops on family trips to enable me to photograph a tree, shrub or forest scene when the light was just right.

Ed Jensen was raised amid the rich farmlands and wooded hills of northwestern Illinois. His love of forests began with a summer job in Olympic National Park during his college years. There he found inspiration in the awesome majesty and subtle beauty of old-growth Douglas-fir/western hemlock forests.

Ed, who retired from Oregon State University at the end of 2014, spent the majority of his career teaching students about forests and the trees and shrubs that comprise them. His enthusiasm for teaching has been recognized with numerous awards and is reflected in several books in addition to this one: *Woody Plants in North America, Trees to Know in Oregon and Washington* and the *Manual of Oregon Trees and Shrubs*. His love of forests has resulted in endearing relationships with thousands of students.